THE
YOUNG
VEGETARIAN'S
COMPANION

THE YOUNG VEGETARIAN'S COMPANION

BY JAN PARR

ILLUSTRATIONS BY SARAH DURHAM

FRANKLIN WATTS
A Division of Grolier Publishing

New York / London / Hong Kong / Sydney
Danbury, Connecticut

Library of Congress Cataloging-in-Publication Data

Parr, Jan.
The Young Vegetarian's Companion / by Jan Parr.
p. cm.
Includes bibliographical references and index.
Summary: Discusses the ethical, religious, health, environmental, and
personal reasons for being a vegetarian and some of the lifestyle issues
involved in this choice.
ISBN 0–531–11277–2 (lib. bdg.)—0–531–15789–x (pbk.)
1. Vegetarianism—Juvenile literature. [1. Vegetarianism.]
I. Title.
TX392.P38   1996
641.5'636—dc20   96–13303
                                                           CIP
                                                           AC

Contents

Acknowledgments

Thanks to all the people who lent their support and expertise to me as I wrote this book. I appreciate all the cooperation and materials I received from the many excellent vegetarian and animal-rights organizations in this country. Specific thanks goes to Karin Horgan Sullivan, senior editor of *Vegetarian Times;* Jeanne Rattenbury; Liz Garfinkle; Sally Clinton, editor of *How on Earth!;* Istvan Nemeth, communications secretary of the Toronto Vegetarian Association; Maxwell Lee of the Vegetarian Society of the United Kingdom; my friends at the Straddle Creek Co-op in Mt. Carroll, Illinois; and my husband, Dan Brinkmeier, who grew up on a cattle farm and who provided me with a valuable perspective. Thanks, too, to my editor, David Strass, for his patience and good suggestions, and to Russell Primm, for making this all happen.

Jan Parr
April 1996

one

INTRODUCTION

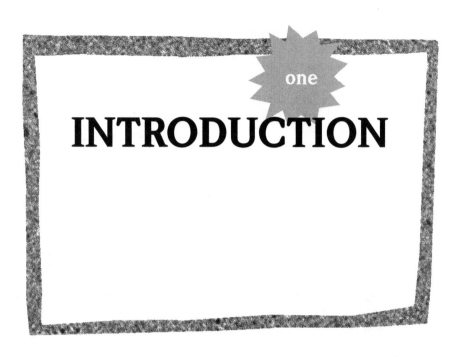

WHAT DO YOU THINK IT MEANS TO BE A VEGETARIAN? Think it means simply not eating meat? That's only part of the story. Being a vegetarian means making a lot of choices about what you eat, about how much you pay attention to your health, about taking control of one part of your life in a positive way, about being sensitive to the conditions of animals, about understanding the balance of life around the world, about sustainable agriculture, and about the well-being of others.

Does it all seem a bit overwhelming? It doesn't need to be. Being a vegetarian is an individual choice, and people are into vegetarianism for a variety of reasons. What's more, those reasons can change and evolve over time. The point is, you can influence many things around you, globally and locally, with a vegetarian lifestyle.

There's never been a better time to be a vegetarian. Once

thought of as a counterculture diet practiced only by hippies, health nuts, or animal rights "extremists," vegetarianism is moving into the mainstream. *Vegetarian Times* magazine estimates that more than 12 million Americans now call themselves vegetarians—about one-third more than a decade ago. In the United Kingdom, actual vegetarians number more than 2.5 million; more than 12 million say they are either vegetarian or don't eat red meat. More than 2 percent of Canadians are vegetarians; many more consider themselves to be vegetarian.

Doctors, major health organizations such as the American Cancer Society and American Dietetic Association, and government agencies such as the Surgeon General's Office are all calling for a drastic reduction in fat intake and for more vegetables, fruits, and whole grains. So what should we eat? Less meat, cheese, and milk, and more of the things vegetarians eat: fruits, vegetables, beans, and grains.

In 1996, for the very first time, the United States government endorsed vegetarian diets in its Dietary Guidelines for Americans. Though these groups don't come right out and advocate vegetarian diets, it's clear that they approve of eating more of the foods these diets contain. In the United States, the National Restaurant Association has recommended that restaurants offer vegetarian items to give people what they want. Big food companies are making veggie burgers and other health-conscious foods and selling them in grocery stores even in small towns.

On the environmental front, many people are realizing that our resources are limited, and that meat production is not the most efficient or most environmentally conscious use of those resources. Factory farming, with its emphasis on treating live animals as commodities to be caged, shot full of hormones and drugs, and cruelly killed, is destroying the family farm and causing a rise in salmonella and other diseases. We need to be concerned about the quality of our food and the treatment of animals. The terrible irony is that starvation around the world continues to increase, as do incidences of cancer, heart disease, and obesity in meat-eating cultures.

Though statistics are hard to come by, the number of vegetarian teenagers is definitely growing. Trend watchers believe that young people make up the fastest-growing segment of vegetarians. All over the country, youths are asking their high schools and colleges to offer vegetarian meals. Teens are organizing animal-rights rallies and joining vegetarian groups. A magazine written by and for teen vegetarians is growing fast. Nearly everyone knows of a neighbor, cousin, or classmate who's vegetarian. A poll conducted by Teenage Research Unlimited showed that one in four teens believes it's "in" to be a vegetarian.

The good news is that not only have vegetarian diets been pronounced "safe" by nearly every major medical authority around, they've even been proven to be healthier than the average meat-eater's diet by countless studies. Vegetarians have been shown to have lower rates of heart disease, less incidence of some cancers, less osteoporosis, and fewer digestive system disorders. Even more good news: a good vegetarian diet is safe for growing teens as well.

Any doubts about whether vegetarian diets can provide strength and vitality can be dispelled by looking at tennis great Martina Navratilova, basketball star Bill Walton, or track legend Carl Lewis—all vegetarians. As for brain power, consider vegetarians in history: Louisa May Alcott, Albert Einstein, Sir Isaac Newton, Henry David Thoreau, George Bernard Shaw, Voltaire, and many others.

WHAT DOES VEGETARIAN MEAN?

Broadly speaking, a vegetarian is someone who doesn't eat meat—any type of meat. But there are many types of vegetarians.

Vegetarian   This is sort of an umbrella term for people who don't eat any meat—no fish, chicken, beef, or pork. Or, as some would say, anything that once had eyes except potatoes. Vegetarians may eat animal products such as milk, cheese, eggs, and honey.

Lacto-ovo vegetarian   Vegetarians who eat eggs (ovo) and milk (lacto) products.

Lacto-vegetarian   A person who eats a vegetarian diet that includes milk products but not eggs.

Ovo-vegetarian   A less common diet that includes eggs but no milk products.

Vegan   (pronounced VEE-gun) or "pure" or "complete" vegetarian. Vegans abstain from all animal products, including all dairy products and honey. Many vegans also do not use leather, silk, goose down, or wool. For the record, the American Vegan Society (AVS) says that only people who do not use animal products for food or clothing should call themselves vegans. The AVS says that "vegan" describes more than just a diet, it's an entire lifestyle that avoids all forms of animal exploitation.

   The vegan lifestyle can be very hard to follow. Some people are strict vegetarians but still use animal products, such as leather shoes or photographic film (manufactured using gelatin from the hooves of cows).

Semi-vegetarian   Many people who call themselves vegetarians eat meat occasionally. They find it hard to pass up turkey at Thanksgiving, say, or they eat a soup with a meat or fish stock (perhaps without knowing it). Strict vegetarians may object to people who are not completely off meat calling themselves vegetarians. Others believe that labels do not matter and that a reduction in meat consumption is certainly desirable.

Terms such as **pollo-vegetarian** (a person who eats no meat except chicken) or **pesco-vegetarian** (eats fish) are somewhat contradictory, because chicken and fish are animals. Whatever people choose to call themselves, it's their business. We should all be happy if people are eating less meat.

Macrobiotic   This diet, which is mostly vegetarian but can also include fish, was developed in Japan. It advocates eating foods that are native to one's area and that balance one another. This diet is often adopted by cancer and AIDS patients who want to make their bodies strong to stave off further damage from disease.

Fruitarians   A person who eats only fruit, seeds, and nuts. Health professionals consider this extreme diet unhealthy and don't recommend it.

More important than any of these labels is the way you treat your body, the approach you take to your life and the planet around you. People are not awarded medals for being vegetarians. You may be criticized or challenged—by non-vegetarians or by strict vegetarians—if you wear leather or order an omelet. The point is, you should take vegetarianism as far as you can or care to. The decision is up to you.

Think it's getting complicated? That's because food is more than just fuel for your body—it's also a social, political, and emotional issue. When you stop eating meat, your parents and other adults may feel as though their lifestyle, traditions, and heritage are being rejected. Many farmers feel as though their very livelihood is being threatened. But food is also a joy, a celebration of life. When you eat with a conscience, knowing the consequences of your diet, food is a true celebration. Vegetarianism can be a positive expression of world conscientiousness and good health.

Why do people become vegetarians? Many people stop eating meat for a variety of ethical reasons. Some are upset by the damage to the environment caused by the production of meat. Others, often called ethical vegetarians, have respect for animals and their right not to suffer for use by humans.

Others are concerned about health. They have seen their fathers and grandfathers have bypass operations. They see overweight, sluggish people everywhere. Eat healthy now, they reason, and they may avoid the health problems faced by their parents.

Some teens are vegetarian for religious reasons. Though few religions ban meat eating or even have much to say about the ethics of animal treatment, some, such as Seventh-Day Adventism, believe that God originally told humans to eat a vegetarian diet to keep their bodies clean and healthy. Many members of some Asian and Indian religions (such as Hindus and Buddhists) are also vegetarian. Buddhists, in particular, preach nonviolence toward all living things. Hindus believe the cow is sacred; some Hindus will eat other kinds of meat, but many do not.

Finally, some people just plain don't like meat—its texture, the blood, the fat, and the way it makes them feel. Taste is an acquired sense, and most people find that after not eating meat for awhile, they lose all craving for it. Some people prefer the "clean" taste of grains, fruits, and vegetables.

For most people who are vegetarian for any length of time the reasons all start to blend together. People who stop eating meat out of respect for animals often find that they feel better and more energetic on their new diet. Or maybe they give up meat out of concern for the environment and later find that they prefer the taste of grains, fruits, and vegetables. Others may first give up meat because of the taste, only to learn later of the other benefits to the environment, their health, and other animals. Soon these convictions become as strong as personal taste preferences. It may be hard to change the world, but taking control over what we put in our mouths is one way to make a difference, however small.

Vegetarians open themselves to a whole new world of food and cultures when they explore Indian, Thai, Middle Eastern, and other cuisines. Most cuisines around the world, in fact, use meat as a condiment, not the centerpiece of a meal. Meatless options abound. You don't have to be a creative culinary whiz to be a vegetarian, but why deny yourself the opportunity to learn new ways to prepare your food? Eating is an important part of life for people everywhere, so learning about food from another culture can reveal a lot about their way of life.

700 MILLION VEGETARIANS

Some teenagers will undoubtedly be accused of becoming vegetarian for the "wrong" reason. Their parents or family friends may believe they are simply following a fad, or rebelling. They may think it's "just a phase." Parents should learn, though, that whatever the reason, a balanced vegetarian diet is a healthy way for teenagers to eat. And if you've gone vegetarian to be rebellious or independent, then it just goes to show that some types of rebellion can be a good thing. This book is intended to give teenagers—and parents—a complete picture of vegetarianism: the history, the politics, the health aspects, the moral and religious aspects, cultural and societal aspescts, and a guide to good vegetarian nutrition for growing kids.

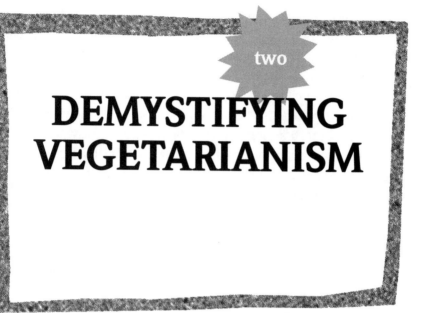

DEMYSTIFYING VEGETARIANISM

two

MISCONCEPTIONS ABOUT VEGETARIANISM ABOUND. Here are the facts that blow them away. Note: this is a handy list to keep around so that you can explain the vegetarian lifestyle to anyone who doesn't understand it—and to anyone who might be interested in joining you.

Vegetarianism is not natural. Human beings were made to eat meat.

This is a tricky one. People have used information about human digestive systems, jaws and teeth, and our ancestors to support either the theory that humans are meant to be omnivores (eating both plant and animal foods) or vegetarians. The debate is far from settled.

Here's the crux of the argument that we were meant to be vegetarian:

- Meat passes very slowly through our digestive system because our small and large intestines are four times longer than those of meat eaters (carnivores). Other primates, such as monkeys and apes, also have long intestines. Because it takes such a long time for meat to digest, it begins to decay in our intestines. Grains, vegetables, and fruits, however, take only about a day and a half to pass through our digestive system.
- Our hands, which are similar to those of apes, are meant for picking foods such as vegetables, fruits, leaves, and flowers, and for gathering seeds and nuts. They were not made for tearing flesh.
- Our lower jaws move up and down and from side to side, like those of a primate. Carnivores' jaws only move up and down.
- We do not have fangs for biting into flesh. Our "canine" teeth are really nothing like those of a dog.
- Carnivores have proportionately larger kidneys and livers than humans. They need these larger organs in order to process the excessive nitrogenous waste of meat.

Some scientists insist that the natural diet of humans is omnivorous, and their evidence can be just as convincing. They argue that our ancestors have eaten meat for millenia and that primates, the animals whose digestive systems are closest to ours, sometimes eat meat. They also argue that nearly all plant eaters—cattle, deer, horses, rhinos—have fermenting vats (enlarged chambers where food sits while microbes attack it to break it down). Humans have no such vat. They also say the presence of salivary glands indicates we could be omnivores, because the acid in saliva helps break down animal proteins.

There are a couple of answers to these arguments. First, though people have eaten meat for thousands of years, a large portion of people throughout history either ate no meat at all or ate it rarely. Yes, people have eaten meat and lived to tell about it. But this does not mean that they need it.

The best response to the myth that people are meant to eat meat is that a diet heavy in meat consumption is not good for our bodies. Perhaps the most important question is not, "Are humans naturally omnivorous?" but rather, "Have humans evolved to the point where they can choose to eat foods that are best for their bodies, their environment, and for their fellow creatures?"

MYTH #2

Vegetarians don't get enough protein.

Not only is it easy to get enough protein from bread, pasta, vegetables, rice, beans, and cereals, but most Americans actually get more protein than they should. This excess protein can cause many serious problems.

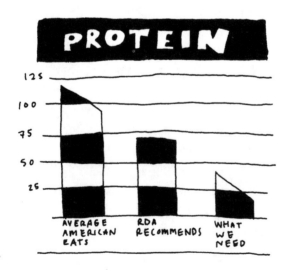

Getting enough protein, the experts say, is simply a matter of getting enough calories. The only foods that have no protein are fruits, sugars, and fats. Few people live on such foods alone. Any vegetarian with an average appetite and a varied diet will get enough protein. If you eat eggs and dairy products, you are probably getting more protein than the government's Recommended Daily Allowance (RDA) suggests. And even though growing teenagers and pregnant women need more protein than other people, it is still easy for them to get the recommended amount.

What is protein for? You might have thought that it provides energy or builds muscle, but it doesn't. Protein helps you to see and think, to make up and repair muscle and bone tissue, to regulate hormones and enzymes, and to fight infections and heal wounds. Protein helps you to digest food and it even affects your genes and chromosomes.

But too much protein can be harmful to your health, and most Americans get too much. The average American consumes 90 to 120 grams of protein per day, two to three times the ideal intake of 20 to 40 grams. Even the U.S. government's RDA suggests, at the highest levels, 63 grams a day, and that number has a built-in safety factor.

What's more, most of this protein is derived from animals, not plants. On average, Americans get two-thirds of their protein from animal products; the other third comes from plants. It is generally the excess animal protein that can cause serious health problems.

MYTH #3

Vegetarians have to plan meals carefully to combine foods for "complete" protein.

Years ago, people thought that one had to combine certain foods in order to get "complete" protein or to make the most of the protein in their foods. This theory was popularized by Frances Moore Lappé in her groundbreaking book, *Diet for a Small Planet.* In it, she spoke of combining rice and beans, grains and cheese, and other foods in order to make a "complete" protein. Protein is made up of nine amino acids—all of which our bodies need. What you need is a balance of amino acids. Rice, for instance, is low in the amino acid called lysine, and beans are low in methionine. Eaten together, rice and beans combine to make "complete" protein with all nine amino acids. But even if you ate nothing but rice or beans (not recommended; you'd have to eat *a lot* of either one), you still would not risk protein deficiency.

Ten years later, in a revised edition of her book, Lappé admitted that she was wrong about protein combining, but still held that to make the best use of protein, you should eat complementary proteins within several hours of one another. Today, scientists know that you only need to obtain all nine amino acids over the course of a day or two, not within a few hours. Since few people eat, say, refried beans without corn chips or tortillas, lentils without rice, or pasta without some grated cheese, these concerns are moot. A normal, varied diet will supply you with all the protein you need.

MYTH #4

Vegetarians can't get vitamin B_{12}.

Because B_{12}—a vitamin essential for keeping your nervous system running correctly—is generally found only in animal products, many people assume that it will be impossible for vegetarians to get it. First of all, only vegans (people who eat no dairy products or eggs) need to worry about B_{12}, since the vitamin is found in eggs, cheese, milk, and yogurt. But your body needs only minuscule amounts of B_{12}, and it can be found in many popular cereals such as Chex, NutriGrain, and Grape-Nuts, and in other prepared foods (take a look at the nutrition information). At least one brand of nutritional yeast also contains B_{12}, and there are B_{12} vitamin supplements (that contain no animal products) as well.

Interestingly, most vitamin B_{12} deficiencies are found in people who eat meat, eggs, milk, and milk products. The bodies of some people just cannot absorb the B_{12}. Vitamin B_{12} deficiencies, then, can come either from a problem with absorption, or from not getting the vitamin in the diet. But the former is more common.

MYTH #5

Vegetarians don't get enough iron.

Studies show that vegetarian teens are no more prone to iron deficiency anemia than meat eaters. But iron deficiency is more common than deficiencies in any other mineral, and it's serious business. It occurs largely because we eat more refined foods these days and no longer cook in cast-iron pots, which add a lot of iron to foods cooked in them.

Pale skin, weakness, shortness of breath, and a lack of appetite are symptoms of iron deficiency. Iron in meat is easier for the body to absorb than the iron in plants (iron-rich plants include greens, other vegetables, and beans). But it is relatively easy to boost your body's absorption of plant iron. Just eat something containing vitamin C when you eat your beans or greens. Tomatoes, oranges, strawberries, grapefruit, and other foods are rich in vitamin C, as are their juices. Vitamin C specifically enhances the absorption of iron from plant sources, partly by reducing ferric iron, which isn't readily ab-

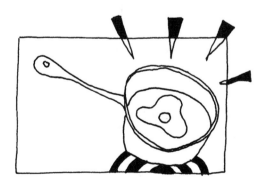

sorbable, to the more absorbable ferrous form. You can also cook food in old-fashioned iron pots to instantly multiply the iron content of your food.

Vegetarians live on salads.

Non-comprehending meat-eaters will often ask, "What *do* you eat?" as if vegetarians have deprived themselves of an incredible array of food choices. But the truth is that many vegetarians eat a wider variety of foods than the typical steak-and-potato American.

All vegetarians are not alike, and not all vegetarians eat the same exact things. But because vegetarianism is about being conscious of what you eat, it often follows naturally that vegetarians become interested in many different sorts of foods. Vegetarianism can open up a whole new world of ethnic cuisine—Mideastern hummus, tabouli, and falafel, Indian curries and dahls, Italian risottos and pastas, Chinese stir-fries and noodles.

Vegetarian meals take a lot more time and effort to prepare.

There are as many types of vegetarians as there are types of meat-eaters. Some people like to spend hours in the kitchen, preparing sauces and marinades for meats, while others exist on frozen dinners and pizzas. Vegetarians are no different. In almost any grocery store these days you can find frozen vegetarian entrées, and all sorts of vegetarian convenience foods such as soups, premade veggie burgers, and pasta sauces.

Of course, it's not healthy to exist on cheese sandwiches, omelets, cheese pizza, and processed or frozen food, so a little cooking knowledge can come in handy. But the same goes for meat eaters: a diet of hamburgers, pepperoni pizza, and frozen dinners is hardly healthy. Once you get your pantry stocked (see chapter eleven), it'll be a snap to spread some refried beans (from a can) on a tortilla, pop it in the microwave, then top with cheese (soy or dairy), shredded lettuce, carrots, diced green peppers, and salsa. Or you can microwave a bag of mixed frozen veggies and mix it with some pasta, canned beans, and a little grated dairy or soy cheese. Within minutes, you have a tasty, nutritious meal.

MYTH #8

Vegetarianism is OK for adults but not for growing kids and teenagers.

Several recent studies have shown that children and teens who are on a vegetarian diet grow as tall and strong as their meat-eating counterparts. Several major medical institutions have stated that vegetarian diets are fine for children and teenagers.

MYTH #9

Vegetarians have to eat cheese and drink milk for strong bones and growth.

Cheese and milk are excellent sources of calcium, which helps build bone. But there are other, nondairy sources of calcium, too, including leafy greens (such as collard and mustard greens), many types of tofu, fortified juices, and soy milk. Not only can you get calcium from sources other than milk, but too much cheese and milk—both of which contain a lot of fat and protein—can even be harmful to your health.

Vegetarians have a hard time living in a meat-eating world. They are social outcasts.

Choosing not to eat meat is getting easier all the time. Though the number of strict vegetarians in most countries may be small, the number of people who are eating less meat and more meatless meals is growing incredibly fast. Most of these people are more interested in their health than they are in animal rights. The American Restaurant Association recently advised member restaurants to offer meatless entrées because a majority of people they surveyed said they liked to see a meatless option on the menu.

Mainstream grocery stores now stock all sorts of vegetarian foods, including soy milk, rice milk, and frozen veggie burgers. Fast-food restaurants are offering veggie burgers. Most major college and university cafeterias are offering veggie fare. Party hosts often ask, as a matter of course, what their guests like to eat. All of this is not to say that vegetarians won't encounter awkward situations—say, Thanksgiving at your grandma's house—but these days, few people think vegetarianism is way out there.

Vegetarianism means depriving yourself.

Many people who eat and enjoy meat believe that everyone has an inherent taste for the stuff. Not so. Many vegetarians, if they once had a taste for meat, lose it, and enjoy other foods as much as anyone. There is a wide array of vegetarian foods to choose from, and most vegetarians see their diet as part of a celebration of food and life, not as depriving themselves of something they want.

Medical science is always coming up with something new. We shouldn't trust them when they say a low-fat diet is healthy. (Also known as the "Next they'll find something wrong with vegetables" myth.)

It may seem that every week we open the newspaper and find another study showing that some food is bad for you and another will cut cholesterol. Then another study comes out and contradicts that advice. But this is no reason to give up on medical science. Yes, the reports often give conflicting information. But there is a consistent message in most medical findings: eat more grains, fruits, and vegetables; eat less fat. Arguments over butter versus margarine, say, are really not the point and are hardly a reason to throw up your hands in despair of finding the "right" way to eat.

Vegetarianism is just a fad.

The 83 percent of India's population who are Hindus, who don't eat beef and are largely vegetarian, would be surprised to hear that vegetarianism is a fad. India has the largest population of vegetarians in the world, and Indian cuisine has the widest range and number of vegetarian dishes. Among Western nations, vegetarianism is clearly a trend, not a fad; one that is gaining more momentum all the time. Meat consumption among people in America, Britain, Canada, and European nations is decidedly down. People are clearly more interested in their health these days, and this is no short-term fad. Twenty years ago, if you'd predicted that large numbers of people would be giving up cigarettes and taking up jogging for their health, few would have believed you. And keep in mind that vegetarianism is certainly not a "new" diet. In fact, the history of vegetarianism dates back to 600 B.C.

three

A HISTORY OF THE VEGETARIAN MOVEMENT

WITH THE RISE IN VEGETARIAN RESTAURANTS, ORGA-nizations, and cookbooks, it may seem to Americans as though vegetarianism was born in this century. But the history of vegetarianism stretches back as early as 600 B.C. Ancient people, too, were concerned about unnecessary slaughter, humane treatment of animals, physical health through diet, and maintaining the earth's natural balance.

Vegetarians throughout history have been a diverse group—they've been Christian fundamentalists, heretics, radical Quakers, humanists, and even a Fascist dictator. In many cases, vegetarians have been persecuted and even killed.

PYTHAGORAS—THE ORIGINAL VEGETARIAN

Before there were such things as "vegetarians" or vegetarian diets, there were Pythagorean societies, named after a sixth-century B.C. philosopher, Pythagoras. Pythagoreans advocated a diet that did not include the flesh of slaughtered animals, but it is not more specific than that. Though Pythagoras himself was most probably a vegan—that is, he ate no animal products whatsoever—historically, the Pythagorean diet included cheese and milk and may also have included fish. The Pythagorean diet forbade beans or any foods that might cause gas or indigestion. It also forbade the eating of plants and animals sacred to the gods. Strict Pythagoreans, then, lived on breads, honey, cereals, fruits, and some vegetables.

Unfortunately, most of what we know about this first vegetarian leader and his philosophy is secondhand, because he did not leave any writings. In fact, all the information we have about Pythagoras comes from two biographers who wrote about him more than two centuries later.

Pythagoras was born on an island off the coast of Turkey and later went to study with the greatest teachers of the time. He became one of the great original thinkers and radically influenced philosophy, science, and mathematics for centuries. Pythagoras was the first Greek to talk about a theory of the soul, which he saw as something immortal that could be transformed time and time again into other living creatures (a theory known as reincarnation or metempsychosis). Because the soul resided in many different hosts, he said, all living things had to be treated equally and with respect.

Pythagoras's followers were called Pythagoreans, but it seems no vegetarian group or movement continued on after the Pythagorean school disbanded around 300 B.C. Pythagorean thought lived on, however, through the philosopher Plato (ca. 428–348 B.C.), who was greatly influenced by the earlier philosopher. We know little of the life of Plato, so it is impossible to know whether he was a vegetarian. We do know, however, that he glorified vegetarianism in his writings. In his famous work, *The Republic*, Plato has Socrates discussing the ideal republic as one in which a vegetarian diet is common. He also warns that eating meat would cause a "fevered state" that will require more doctors, more territory to support the increased food requirement, and an army to acquire and defend this territory. The inevitable consequence of these conditions, he theorized, would be war. (How right he turned out to be!) In another of his famous "Dialogues," Plato describes a pure vegetarian diet as divinely ordained.

EARLY ADVOCATES OF VEGETARIANISM

The next important vegetarian figure in history was Plutarch (A.D. 46–120), a Greek writer, biographer, essayist, and historian. Plutarch is significant in that he was the first Greek writer who did not link his vegetarianism with the concept of transmigration of the soul, or reincarnation. Instead, Plutarch argued that humans are not naturally flesh eaters in the sense that they are physically unlike carnivores. Humans do not have beaks, sharp talons or claws, or pointed teeth. He pointed out that the digestive systems of humans are not made to process meat—human intestines are twisted and long, instead of short and straight like those of carnivores.

Plutarch believed that eating meat made humans' thoughts muddled and not sharp. He also protested against the cruel treatment of animals in preparing them for slaughter. "It is best to accustom one's self to eat no flesh at all," he wrote, "for the earth affords plenty enough of things fit not only for nourishment, but for delight and enjoyment."

Porphyry, born A.D. 232 in Phoenicia, wrote what is believed to be the earliest surviving book on vegetarianism. *Abstinence from Animal Foods* was written in four books. The first was in the form of a letter to a friend who had gone back to eating meat after being a vegetarian. The second condemns animal sacrifice. The third discusses the concept of justice and implores us to extend it toward animals. Porphyry argued that animals are capable of sophisticated reasoning and have some ability to understand verbal commands and sounds. The fourth is a discussion of dietary habits. Like Pythagoras and Plutarch, Porphyry believed that eating meat created a violent and aggressive personality.

When we move into the age of Christianity, we find much less tolerance for vegetarianism in the West. Though evidence suggests that the very early Christian church may have been mostly vegetarian, that movement ended with Paul the missionary, who became Paul the Apostle. Paul widened the Church to include gentiles. In the process, he refrained from making rules about diet, because in order to convert people he believed he had to have as few rules as possible.

Meat eating was seen by Christians as part of the glory of God and one of the delights that the Lord had given both to nourish humans and to give them pleasure. Meat also came to stand for wealth and social position. Only the poor, who could not afford it, did not eat meat. In fact, to make a choice not to eat meat was considered heresy (an opinion different from that of the church's teachings), and heretics were often put to death. As a result, vegetarians tended to keep quiet about their eating habits.

In the sixty or so biographies of the great painter, engineer, scientist, and musician Leonardo da Vinci (1452–1519), only one book mentions his vegetarianism, even though he considered it a central part of his life. In his notebooks he writes, "Now does not nature produce enough simple vegetarian food for thee to satisfy thyself?" He also expressed his thoughts on vegetarianism in his paintings, not just his writings. In the landscapes of his great paintings, and the studies of rocks and water, we can see that Leonardo believed there was life and energy in everything—clouds, stones, pebbles, torrents, and light. His painting "The Virgin of the Rocks" (ca. 1485), for example, places the infants John and Christ with Mary and an angel in a garden-like setting. The subjects are sitting comfortably beside a pool, and the plants and mist around them simultaneously lend a sense of mystery and ease to the religious theme. Such a belief goes back to the philosophers before Socrates, who saw the spirit in everything.

MODERN VEGETARIANISM

The modern-day vegetarian movement in the West was started in England in the seventeenth century. Around this time, people began to change their thinking about animals and objected to the exploitation of animals for human use. During this period, several religious sects such as the Ratners, Judaists, and later the Southcottians and Swedenborgians all had diets that excluded animal foods.

A famous vegetarian of the time was Thomas Tryon (1634–1703), who wrote one of the first vegetarian cookbooks. His *Bill of Fare of Seventy-Five Noble Dishes of Excellent Food* was published in 1691. It doesn't really resemble today's cookbooks, though. In fact, most early vegetarian cookbooks tended to be more like essays trying to convince readers of the rightness of vegetarianism. (The first modern vegetarian cookbook, *Science in the Kitchen,* was written by Ella Kellogg, wife of cereal magnate John Harvey Kellogg, in the early 1900s.)

The British Romantic poet Percy Bysshe Shelley (1792–1822) was an outspoken vegetarian who wrote about the practice in his first long poem, *Queen Mab*. He also translated some of Plutarch's essays on vegetarianism and wrote "The Vegetable System of Diet."

Until the 1840s, the term "vegetarianism" was still not in use, though it was coined around 1830. The Pythagorean diet officially became the vegetarian diet in 1847, when the Vegetarian Society was founded in England. Years later a president of the society explained that the name was derived from the Latin *vegetus,* meaning "vigorous and lively."

Organizers of the Vegetarian Society were particularly influenced by the work of Justus Liebig, a German chemist who had concluded that there was no difference between plant and animal protein. (We now know that's not quite true.) Liebig's studies seemed to provide, for the first time, scientific evidence that a vegetarian diet was safe and healthy.

Meanwhile, vegetarian groups were forming in other countries. In the mid-1800s, three members of the Vegetarian Society—Reverend William Metcalfe, Sylvester Graham (for whom graham flour and graham crackers are named), and Bronson Alcott (the father of Louisa May Alcott, who wrote *Little Women*) emigrated to the United States from England. In 1850 they organized the American Vegetarian Convention in New York. The German Vegetarian Society was founded in 1867 by Eduard Baltzer.

Back in England, Henry Salt, a scholar and master at Eton College, founded the Humanitarian League in 1891, one of the first major animal-rights groups. Salt, who was friends with other notable vegetarians of the time—playwright George Bernard Shaw and the spiritual leader Mohandas K. Gandhi—formed the league to fight injustice, inequality, and cruelty to all creatures.

Gandhi traveled to England in 1888 and found a vegetarian restaurant in London. It was at this restaurant that he found books and essays that particularly influenced him, such as Henry Salt's *A Plea for Vegetarianism*. Salt's suggestion to link the abstinence from meat with greater social reforms was an idea that appealed to Gandhi. Gandhi later became a member of the London Vegetarian Society and wrote many articles for its journals.

Vegetarian literature often made the claim that eating meat made people aggressive (and vegetarianism made people more peaceful), but at least one historical figure blew this theory out of the water. Much evidence suggests that Adolf Hitler was a vegetarian. According to historian Colin Spencer, Hitler wanted to be set apart from other people, to feel superior to meat eaters. He was also greatly influenced by the vegetarianism of his hero, the German composer Richard Wagner. Spencer believes that Hitler may have eaten meat occasionally prior to 1931, but that after his beloved niece was shot dead that year he never touched it again. It may be hard for today's vegetarians to understand how a person with such a low regard for human life could have been a vegetarian.

You might think that the vegetarian movement in Germany would have gained a lot of momentum under Hitler, but the opposite was true. For one thing, the German authorities did not want Hitler to be associated with "common groups." Hitler thought his vegetarianism set him apart from the average German. Also, Nazis generally tried to suppress any group over which they didn't have control, so they declared vegetarian societies illegal, and a vegetarian magazine in Frankfurt ceased publication in 1933. Most vegetarians kept quiet about their diet. If they knew about Hitler's preferences they kept quiet about that, too, instead of using the knowledge to gain strength for their movement.

Though they were not allowed to organize, the German people kept their vegetarian practices. In 1939, when rationing began during World War II, vegetarians were allowed to exchange meat credits for dairy credits. Eighty-three thousand people registered as vegetarians.

After the war, vegetarian literature stopped making the claim that eating meat led to aggression and that wars could be ended if people stopped slaughtering animals for food. The idea of the vegetarian as pacifist and humanist, embodied in a figure such as Gandhi, was put aside after the revelation that Hitler was a vegetarian.

RECENT VEGETARIAN HISTORY

Beginning in the 1970s, the vegetarian movement exploded, largely in the United Kingdom, United States, and Canada. In 1976, Frances Moore Lappé published *Diet for a Small Planet,* a book that made readers aware of the connection between food, animal rights, world hunger, and the allocation of natural resources. *Diet for a Small Planet* was an instant best-seller and has influenced a great many Americans. Peter Singer, a very influential modern-day philosopher on animal rights, wrote *Animal Factories* and *Animal Rights.* His work brought to light many of the inhumane practices at the heart of factory farming.

A magazine devoted to vegetarianism, *Vegetarian Times,* began in 1974 and thrives today, along with several other vegan and vegetarian publications, including one specifically for young vegetarians (*How on Earth!*). The American Vegan Society was founded in 1960 and the North American Vegetarian Society in 1974. People for the Ethical Treatment of Animals (PETA) was founded in 1980. Today there are hundreds of vegetarian societies in the United States, the United Kingdom, and Canada. What all this spells is an increased awareness of, and interest in, world peace, sustainable agriculture, and personal health. And it shows no sign of stopping.

four

SAVE THE ENVIRONMENT

TELL SOMEONE YOU'RE A VEGETARIAN FOR ENVIRON-
mental reasons and wait for the response: "What does eating meat
have to do with the environment?" The answer: everything. Most
people are often unaware of the effects their diet has on their bodies, other humans, other living things, and the planet.

The demand for meat and the production of that meat—from
growing feed for animals to animal grazing to the increasing number
of livestock that roam this earth—have harmed our environment in
many ways. These include the destruction of Central American rain
forests, topsoil depletion and erosion, the consumption of limited natural resources such as land and water, and water and air pollution.
We'll look at each one of these issues in this chapter.

DESTRUCTION OF RAIN FORESTS

Tropical rain forests are important for our survival in several ways,
and the production of meat is rapidly destroying the forests. Rain

forests are often called "the earth's lungs" because they provide a substantial part of the earth's oxygen. Eight percent of the planet's land vegetation is found in rain forests, and more species of plant and animal life are found there than on all the rest of the earth. Nearly one-quarter of all medications and pharmaceuticals come from tropical plants.

So what does meat production have to do with the rain forest? Cattle ranchers are clearing large sections of the rain forest to establish grazing lands. It takes 55 square feet (5 sq m) of rain forest

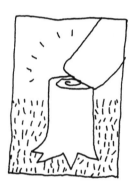

for each quarter-pound hamburger made from cattle imported from Central America. Between 1966 and 1983, some 40,000 square miles (104,000 sq km) of Amazon rain forests were cleared by the Brazilian government, and estimates are that 38 percent of that land was used for large-scale cattle developments. Cutting these trees down has caused the destruction of many species of animals and plants and the creation of carbon dioxide pollution, a major

factor in the "greenhouse effect." The connection between rain forest destruction and possible contributions to global warming, therefore, is linked to meat production.

GLOBAL WARMING

Commercial cattle ranching contributes to global warming in several ways. First, forests are being cleared to create additional grazing ground for cattle. The burning of the earth's biomass (plants, trees, shrubs) is a major cause of global warming. When plants and trees die or are burned, the carbon they have stored up is emitted into the atmosphere. Millions of acres of Central American forests have been destroyed to make room for cattle grazing. In 1987, at the peak of a clearing and burning binge in the forests of the Amazon, some

1.2 billion tons of carbon dioxide (CO_2) were released into the atmosphere. In that year, the deforestation of the Amazon rain forest alone contributed 9 percent of total worldwide carbon dioxide to global warming from all sources.

Second, modern cattle ranching consumes energy. It takes 22 to 40 times less fossil fuel to produce grain and beans than it does to produce meat and dairy products. The fuel runs tractors and other equipment needed to plant and harvest feed for the animals and pump water. It also takes energy to produce fertilizers and pesticides for feed crops. The burning of fossil fuels emits carbon dioxide into the air, which contributes to global warming. It takes more than 260 gallons (984 l) of fuel to provide beef for the average family of four for a year. When that fuel is burned, it releases 2.5 tons of carbon dioxide into the atmosphere—as much as the average car emits in six months.

Third, modern farmers use a lot of petrochemical fertilizers on the crops they feed their cattle, and these fertilizers emit nitrous oxide, yet another of the greenhouse gases. The use of chemical fertilizers has skyrocketed over the past forty years: we were using 143 million tons in 1989, up from 14 million tons in 1950. Nitrous oxide is emitted from other sources, as well, but nitrous oxide emitted from all sources accounts for 6 percent of the global warming effect.

Fourth, cattle and the production of cattle feed account for an increase in methane gas emissions over the past several decades. Why is methane so bad? One methane molecule can trap 25 times as much heat from the sun as a molecule of CO_2. Methane gases now make up 18 percent of the global warming effect, but some scientists believe that methane will become the primary global warming gas over the next fifty years. Methane gas also comes from peat bogs, rice paddies, and landfills, but the increase in cow population and land to feed them account for much of the increase. Cows themselves emit methane gas when they expel intestinal gases (about 12 percent of all the methane released into the atmosphere). What's more, when forests and grasslands are burned to make way for cattle-grazing pasture, that burning foliage turns into methane gas that's released into the atmosphere.

LAND USE

Production of meat and other animal products (milk, cheese, butter) takes up a large percentage of the earth's land. Cattle and other livestock that graze, such as sheep and goats, chomp their way through one-half of the earth's total land area. Additional grain for these animals and pigs and poultry is grown on one-fourth of the world's cropland. More than 90 percent of all agricultural land in the United States—representing more than half of the total land area of the continental United States—is dedicated to the production of meat and animal products. This includes land not just for grazing cattle but also for growing corn, hay, and soybeans as feed for the animals. All other farming, including plant food for humans, cotton, and tobacco, uses only 10 percent of the United States's agricultural land. In the United Kingdom, 38 million acres (15.3 million ha) of land, or more than 80 percent of the total, are used either directly or indirectly for meat and dairy production. Cattle and sheep graze on 60 percent of the land in Australia.

TOPSOIL LOSS

Topsoil is that few inches of soil found on the top of land. It contains a lot of the life and nutrients necessary to grow crops. Today, the United States is losing land to soil erosion much faster than new soil is being created. Even under the best circumstances, experts say it takes thirty to one hundred years for the earth to produce an inch of new topsoil. Others say it takes as long as three hundred years. That's because the process of creating topsoil—basically the chemical breakdown of plant roots, fossils, leaves, insects, and other organisms—is an extremely slow one. Yet an inch of topsoil can be lost in a matter of decades, years, or even hours in some areas. Some three million acres (1.2 million ha) of land is being lost to livestock agriculture each year. Some experts are predicting cropland shortages in the United States by the year 2000.

The United Nations Environmental Program estimates that the world loses 25 billion tons of topsoil each year. This loss of topsoil makes croplands less productive. Experts estimate that the productivity of the world's croplands has diminished by almost a third in recent years. For every inch of topsoil lost to erosion, experts estimate, the amount of grain a farmer can get from the land goes down 6 percent. The Worldwatch Institute estimates that the loss of 25 billion tons of topsoil worldwide each year has reduced the annual world grain harvest by a comparable 6 percent—a loss of 9 million tons of grain per year.

Cattle contribute directly to topsoil loss by trampling the ground over and over again. The soil they tramp down becomes compacted and hard, especially if there is clay in it. Then, when it rains, this compacted soil is less able to absorb water, so the water simply runs off the land, taking the top layer of soil with it. Cattle also eat all the perennial grasses (grasses that normally come back year after year), and this allows weeds and tougher shrubs to spread. The new weeds do not anchor the topsoil as well as the grasses, so wind and rain can take it away more easily.

Topsoil loss is not only a result of overgrazing, but also of deforestation and planting too many crops to feed animals. How much topsoil erosion can be attributed directly to cattle and to the production of crops to feed them? No one is sure, but one researcher estimates nearly 6 billion of the 7 billion tons of eroded soil in the United States is the fault of cattle and production of their feed crops.

Soil erosion is the most serious environmental problem facing Australia, affecting nearly two-thirds of the continent's arable land (land that is suitable for growing crops). Soil loss and spreading desertification (the reduction of dry land's ecological productivity) is the biggest threat to the environment on the African continent as well.

Topsoil loss is seriously affecting the productivity of rangeland and cropland in Asia, India, and Central and South America as well.

Grazing cattle in the West are directly responsible for contributing to the endangerment of several species of plants and animals, to the destruction of natural habitats, and to the deterioration of the land. And the U.S. government admits as much. A 1989 report issued by the National Wildlife Federation and the Natural Resources Defense Council found that 68 percent of the 138 million Bureau of Land Management acres recently inventoried were, by the agency's own definition, in "unsatisfactory" condition. "Poor livestock grazing practices continue to be endemic to the vast majority of those lands," the report said.

Cattle trample native plants and destroy the organisms— bacteria, protozoa, fungi, algae, insects, earthworms, and mice—that live in the top two inches of soil, where they play a critical part in maintaining soil fertility and building new soil. The hooves and mouths of cattle also destroy native flora and fauna, eliminating the plant cover that provides birds, insects, and other mammals with food and shelter.

DEPLETION OF WATER SOURCES

A Californian restricted to watering her lawn or washing his car for only a couple of hours a day might be surprised by this: One of the main reasons for water shortages in the United States is the production of beef. Nearly half the water consumed in the United States goes to grow feed for cattle and other livestock. It takes hundreds of gallons of water to produce just one pound (0.45 kg) of grain-fed steak. Frances Moore Lappé noted that "the water used to produce

just ten pounds (4.5 kg) of steak equals the household consumption of [her] family for an entire year." As *Newsweek* magazine put it, "the water that goes into a 1,000-pound (454 kg) steer would float a destroyer." But striking analogies aside, it takes up to fifteen times more water to produce a pound of beef protein than it does to produce the same amount of plant protein.

Nearly half the grain-fed cattle in the United States rely on a single underground water source, called an aquifer, that runs under midwestern and western states. It's called the Ogallala aquifer, and it is one of the world's great underground reserves, stretching from northwestern Texas to South Dakota. In the last forty years, a total of 120 cubic miles (500 cubic km) of water have been taken from this reserve. This water will not be replaced. To put the amount into perspective, consider that, each year, farmers take more water from the Ogallala than the annual flow of the Colorado River. Hydrologists estimate that the aquifer is already half depleted in Kansas, Texas, and New Mexico.

The water depletion situation is worst in California, where 42 percent of the irrigation water is used for livestock production. Water tables in the state have dropped so low that the earth itself is shrinking under the vacuum. Some 5,000 square miles (13,000 sq km) of the San Joaquin Valley have sunk, in some places by as much as 29 feet (9 m).

ACID RAIN

Too much manure is a real problem! The land can absorb only so much of it at a time. For example, Dutch farms produce 94 million tons of manure every year, but their land can absorb only 50 million tons. The rest of it has to be dealt with in some way. Illegal dumping has become common. These dumps produce clouds of ammonia that poison trees and plants. Some scientists believe that ammonia is a primary source of acid rain. According to the Dutch National Institute of Public Health and Environmental Protection, the ammonia that livestock discharge into the air is the single largest source of acid dropped on Dutch soil—doing more damage than the country's cars or factories. The Netherlands, Belgium, and France all are producing more manure than their land can absorb.

WATER POLLUTION

Manure nitrogen, mixed with nitrogen from artificial fertilizers, finds its way through the soil into underground water tables. There it becomes nitrates, which can cause all sorts of health problems for humans, such as nervous-system damage and cancer. Water in most countries of western Europe is contaminated by nitrates, and in the United States, about one-fifth of the wells in livestock states such as Iowa, Kansas, and Nebraska have nitrate levels that are considered unsafe.

American livestock contribute five times more harmful organic waste to water pollution that do people, and twice that of industry, estimates the writer George Borgstrom.

WILD WEST WELFARE

Raising cattle in any part of the world has its destructive effects. But it's even worse in areas where the land is not very good to begin with. Cattle ranching in the western United States makes little sense. It is dry, there are few plants for cattle to graze on, and there are many predators that stalk and kill cattle, such as coyotes. In Florida, where the climate is moist, you can raise enough plants for one cow on 1 acre (0.4 ha) of ground. Compare that with Montana, where you may need at least 100 acres (40 ha), or with Nevada, where you'll need about 220 acres (90 ha). Unless you hire herders or have guard dogs, losing cattle to wolves and other predators is a real threat. What's more, it's expensive to bring the necessary water to this land: western cattle operations require pipelines, windmills, stock ponds, and irrigation systems.

Why, then, do people raise cattle out west? The answer is simple: because they are subsidized by U.S. tax dollars. In 1989, livestock ranchers leased 267 million acres (417,000 sq mi; 1 million sq km) of Bureau of Land Management and U.S. Forest Service land in the West. These ranchers paid $35 million for the public lands they used that year, about one-sixth what they might have paid to lease private land. Grazing fees for the same year covered less than 45 percent of what it cost the federal government to pay for range management and improvement.

Let's look at one example of the subsidies ranchers receive. A rancher might pay an annual fee of $18,000 for the use of 126,000 acres (51,000 ha) of public land. To help lessen the environmental impact of cattle grazing on the land, the Bureau of Land Management will build a water pipeline, drill a well, and put up 16 miles (25 km) of fence—all at a cost of about $174,000. The rancher may be required to pay part of the costs or donate his labor, but the major expenses are paid for by the public.

In this scenario, let's estimate that maintenance of the pipeline costs $14,000 per year. Though the American taxpayers have paid for most of these improvements, they will receive only half of the $18,000 annual fee in return. By law, half of all grazing fees must be used to finance more "improvements" such as the pipeline. Another 12 percent goes to the county grazing board. In the end, the public treasury receives only $6,800—about five cents per acre. By law, farmers are required to repay the costs for constructing irrigation systems, but the government's General Accounting Office found in 1981 that farmers have repaid only 8 percent of the costs to the federal government.

Livestock haven't always been a drain on our environment. Decades ago, when global meat consumption was much lower, farm animals were an important part of a balanced ecological system.

Their manure returned nutrients to the soil, they grazed on fields that were not in use, and they provided power to pull farm equipment and carry goods to market. In India, livestock are used to carry about half of all goods to market. What's more, manure was used as fuel (and still is in rural India) and as a material to strengthen the walls of mud homes. Cattle and sheep traditionally ate grass and crop wastes on farms. Pigs and fowl, which cannot digest grass, ate crop wastes, kitchen scraps, and whatever else they could find. In a nutshell, domestic animals used to contribute to a balanced agricultural environment.

During the past fifty years, the balance has been disturbed because the number of livestock has soared. As demand for meat has increased, farmers have discovered ways to get more and more grain out of an acre of land. This has made corn and barley a relatively inexpensive way to feed animals. As the number of people demanding meat (and those who can afford it) increases, meat production around the world has soared, nearly quadrupling since 1950. The United States is the meat-eating capital of the world, with per-person consumption around 250 pounds (112 kg) a year.

As a result, intensive, specialized meat, egg, and dairy farms have spread like wildfire. Livestock operations have caused considerable damage to the environment with no end in sight.

The production of meat is vastly inefficient. For every 16 pounds (7 kg) of grain and soy fed to beef cattle in the United States, only one pound of meat is produced. So why not eliminate the middle man? (In this case, the cow.) It's a concept referred to as "eating low on the food chain." The idea is to eat the grain that feeds the cow instead of eating the cow itself.

five

SAVE THE ANIMALS:
ETHICAL AND RELIGIOUS ARGUMENTS

DO ANIMALS HAVE RIGHTS? WHAT ARE OUR DUTIES to them? These are questions that have been pondered for hundreds—even thousands—of years. First, no ethical debate can take place unless we first decide whether eating the flesh of animals is necessary for human health. After all, if we had to eat meat in order to live, then there'd be little reason to talk about the ethics of killing animals for food. As we will see in later chapters, though, plant foods provide us with all the nourishment we need. How, then, can the killing of animals be justified? In this chapter we will explore what major philosophers, scholars, and religious thinkers have had to say about the treatment of animals.

One modern vegetarian thinker, Keith Akers, author of *A Vegetarian Sourcebook,* argues that we can take two positions in justifying killing animals for food. One, we can deny that animals suffer. Two, we can admit they suffer but claim that the benefits of eating meat outweigh the ethical drawbacks.

The first position can be soundly refuted. Chapter six will illustrate the horrendous conditions under which animals raised for food are kept today. Factory farms cram animals together in cages so small that they can't turn around. Pigs and chickens are driven mad by these conditions and resort to attacking each other. Many suffer from disease, depression, and severe neurosis. It is not conscionable to argue that animals raised for food do not suffer.

A variety of ethical (secular) and moral (religious) arguments refute the second position, that the benefits outweigh the drawbacks. People in many cultures have thought hard about what it means to kill animals for food or other ends, and they have concluded that it is preferable to treat animals with respect and deference.

Are animals our fellow creatures? As Akers points out, they are like us in many ways: they have a sense of sight, taste, touch, smell, and hearing. They can communicate and can experience emotions such as fear and excitement. So if they are such sentient beings, how can one justify doing them harm? We must explore the explanations for this justification in order to fully understand the ethical debate. Keith Akers describes three main arguments in defense of the killing of animals.

ARGUMENT 1

Killing for food is natural.

Animals kill other animals, don't they? So in the order of nature, some animals are food for us. This argument can justify hunting for subsistence. Hunting for survival, however, is not as prevalent as the current system of raising and killing animals for food that we have today. If the practice of killing is defended on the grounds that it is natural, then it has to happen naturally. For instance, in the wild, animals hunt only select and isolated members of

a herd, particularly those who are sick and weak. On today's farms, nearly every animal of the herd is wiped out. This practice is anything but natural. Some may then argue that there is no difference between hunting and slaughter, but they cannot claim that the slaughter is a part of nature, as hunting for subsistence could be considered.

Is it ethically more acceptable, then, for a person to eat meat he or she has hunted? Most vegetarians would argue that killing is always wrong, and that animals have a right to live. But we've already said that animals kill other animals, so why shouldn't humans do the same? Well, we can draw a distinction between unnecessary and necessary killing. Humans have options; they don't have to kill animals for food. There are plenty of other options from the plant world. A tiger or wolf knows of no other way to get food. If "nature" here refers to the best way to survive, and if we can survive without hunting, then we can argue that it is more natural not to kill animals for food.

ARGUMENT 2

Animals are significantly different from people, so it's acceptable to kill them.

The philosopher David Hume (1711–1776) believed that humans are vastly superior to animals. So, he argued, animals do not deserve any sort of justice. But most people can see where this sort of thinking could logically lead: anyone who is "inferior" does not deserve justice. Therefore slavery, racism, colonialism, and infanticide (the killing of babies, especially baby girls) are justified. One animal-rights philosopher, Peter Singer, calls Hume's sort of thinking "speciesism." Like racism or sexism, speciesism discriminates against animals because they are different or "inferior."

46

Hume was not alone. Another philosopher, Immanuel Kant, said in a lecture in 1780, "So far as animals are concerned, we have no direct duties. Animals are not self-conscious, and are there merely as a means to an end. That end is man." His thoughts reflected the utilitarian trend that was based in part on the ideas developed by Saint Thomas Aquinas more than five hundred years earlier. Aquinas was a realist, and he argued that reason makes us superior to animals. By his thinking, animals are not rational and, therefore, we don't have an obligation to be charitable to them. There are many flaws in such an argument.

First, perhaps animals are more rational than we know. Second, isn't the ability to *feel* more important in any case? As Jeremy Bentham put it in his 1781 book *Introduction to the Principles of Morals and Legislation,* "The question is not, 'Can they reason?' nor 'Can they talk?' but, 'Can they suffer?'" Most scientists agree that animals feel pain and sadness and develop emotional attachments with one another. Scientists have proven that whales have a sort of "language" they use to communicate with one another and with humans. Perhaps animals are not so different from us after all.

ARGUMENT 3

Abstaining from killing is absurd.

This argument makes the case that we kill living things all the time, such as insects and plants. Isn't it hypocritical, then, to say that it is ethically wrong to kill an animal? Some people do attempt to lead a lifestyle that prevents injury to animals, if not plants. The Jains, for example, a religious sect, had servants brush the path in front of them so as not to step on any insects, and they often wore cloths over their mouths to keep from inhaling a hapless bug. What's more, they did not eat root vegetables (vegetables that grow out of the ground, such as potatoes, turnips, and carrots) because many insects would be killed digging the food out of the earth.

True, actively avoiding the killing of even the smallest insect can really hamper one's lifestyle! But aside from such accidents or "acts of God" or whatever you wish to call them, it is simply not necessary to kill animals. The most straightforward response to the suggestion that killing is unavoidable, then, is to point out the drastic difference between killing an intruder, such as a roach or fly, and going out of your way to kill an innocent animal, such as a cow, that would otherwise be harmless and which you do not need to eat in order to survive.

But, as they say, death is still a part of life. Setting aside for the moment the horrors of the modern factory farm, let's say that farms were more humane and the system was reformed so that animals were treated well, allowed to roam about in green pastures for years until they were slaughtered (as humanely and painlessly as possible) for meat. Would it then be ethically acceptable to kill them for food? Not if you buy the arguments stated above that killing animals for food is wrong.

The argument that animals suffer can extend beyond the killing of animals to their way of life. Lacto-ovo vegetarians—the majority of vegetarians—eat products that come from animals that might suffer just as much, if not more, than animals raised specifically for slaughter. And most dairy cows and laying hens end up at the slaughterhouse anyway. Well, the lacto-ovo vegetarian can answer that humans do not *have* to harm or cause the death of any animal in order to obtain food such as eggs or milk. Some lacto-ovo vegetarians get their eggs and milk from free-range animals that are allowed to wander uncaged. Some vegetarian activists argue that it would be more humane to eat an animal killed in the wild or a fish caught in a stream than to drink a glass of milk produced under the current factory-farm system.

Yet another philosophical position one could take toward animals: The conscientious omnivore (a person who eats both plant and animal foods) is basically a meat eater with a conscience. He or she admits that causing pain to animals is wrong but believes that an instantaneous, painless death at the end of a normal animal life is morally acceptable. Some of these people live on farms, eating only animals that they themselves have raised humanely or wild animals they have killed. Ethical vegetarians might still object to this sort of logic, but at least conscientious omnivores admit that animals are entitled to some kind of consideration.

ANIMAL RIGHTS: WORLD RELIGIONS

Unfortunately, few religions have much to say about the treatment of animals. Many cultures have, however, developed belief systems that include specific rules about eating. The reasons vary greatly, and the rules themselves can be complicated, but nevertheless some religions restrict the eating of animals. Curiously, only the Jains have a doctrine (written rules) that forbids the eating of meat. In other religions, culture, economics, and history have played a role in the vegetarian practices of members. Still others have little or nothing to say about the rights of animals, and some say it's wrong to consider treating animals as humanely as humans. Which religions would an ethical vegetarian be most comfortable with? Here are discussions of the role of diet and animal rights in a number of world religions.

Hinduism

The foundation of this ancient religion, which originated in India and is still practiced there, is a belief in many gods, and the acceptance of reincarnation (living many lives) and karma. Karma is the concept that your behavior in past lives has affected your current life, and behavior in this life will affect your future lives. For this reason, Hindus preach kindness to all fellow beings including animals, and in particular, the cow.

Why is the cow sacred and not other animals? There's nothing in doctrine about the cow, so the origin of this belief is uncertain. Some myths state that Brahma created cows to provide *ghee* (clarified butter) for use in priestly ceremonies. Others point to the *Bhagwat Prana,* a book about the life of Krishna written in the fifth century and translated into Hindi in the fifteenth century. In it, Krishna describes the cow as the "cow mother" of every Hindu, and from then on no orthodox Hindu killed a cow or ate beef. Vegetarianism has a long history within Hinduism, dating back many centuries before Christ. But not all Hindus are vegetarian. Many, in fact, eat mutton, kid, and fish.

Today in North America, the "Hare Krishnas," members of the International Society for Krishna Consciousness, founded in 1966, are all vegetarian followers of the Hindu tradition.

Buddhism

Like Hinduism, Buddhism originated in India and incorporates the belief in many gods, karma, and reincarnation. Buddhists reject the notion of a self or soul. They believe that the path of life is essentially suffering, and that the cause of suffering is desire. The path to salvation, then, is to give up all desire.

There are two branches of Buddhism: Theravada and Mahayana. Theravada, the older, original religion, is practiced in Myanmar, Sri Lanka, Laos, Thailand, Cambodia, Tibet, and Malaysia. Mahayana is practiced in China. Meat eating is considered acceptable in Theravada but is looked down on in Mahayana. The reasons are not based in doctrine but in differences in rituals through which the two groups of monks receive their food. In Theravada, monks beg for food and must accept what is given to them. But such a monk may not eat meat that is specially killed or prepared for him. Mahayana monks don't beg for food and are strictly vegetarian.

50

Many Buddhist laypeople in China are also vegetarians. When laypeople receive ordination, they must take one to five vows, the first of which is to not take the life of any sentient (feeling) creature. Most people take this to mean vegetarianism, but some argue that it means only that one cannot personally slaughter animals or eat an animal killed specifically for one's benefit. Modern Japanese Buddhist leaders have not established a position on the subject, saying only that it is a "reality" that people kill plants and animals.

Jainism

The Jain religion is the only one that expressly forbids eating meat. This religion, which came into being about the same time as Buddhism (around the sixth century B.C.), shares the acceptance of the ideas of reincarnation, karma, and nonviolence with Buddhists and Hindus. The Jains believe there is life in everything—even rocks and stones—and that, as much as possible, one should refrain from violence toward any "living" thing.

There is a hierarchy of beings according to the Jains, and it is worse to do harm to a higher being than to a lower being. The beings are divided by the number of senses they possess, from five-sensed beings (humans, gods, infernal beings, some animals) to one-sensed beings, or *nigodas* (vegetable, earth, water, fire, and wind bodies, which possess only the sense of touch). In any case, however, Jains believe it is ideal not to cause harm to any kind of being, even the lowest.

Jains may not consume meat, alcohol, honey, or some types of figs, because *nigodas* are present in the fermentation and sweetening process. For the Jains, vegetarianism is grounded in the necessity of purifying the soul and its attachment to matter. Denial of the body and purification of the soul are most important; nonviolence toward other beings is an important secondary consideration.

Judaism

In general, Judaism has considered meat eating as a totally justified indulgence. But the humane treatment of animals has always been a central part of Judaism. An important book written in the nineteenth century by Aaron Frankel, called *Thou Shall Not Kill, or the Torah of Vegetarianism,* prompted the formation of numerous Jewish vegetarian societies around the world.

According to the Book of Genesis, the first diet of humanity was vegetarian—even animals were to be vegetarian: "God also said, 'I give you all plants that bear seed everywhere on earth, and every tree bearing fruit which yields seed: they shall be yours for food. All green plants I give for food to the wild animals, to all the birds of heaven, and to all reptiles on earth, every living creature'" (Genesis 1:29–31).

After Noah and the flood, however, meat eating was permitted: "Every creature that lives and moves shall be food for you; I give you them all, as once I gave you all green plants. But you must not eat the flesh with the life, which is the blood, still in it" (Genesis 9:3–4). What are we to make of this apparent reversal? Some people argue that the original diet was the one that God intended us to have, and that He later allowed meat only when He saw that humans were going to disobey His original orders.

The Bible calls for humans to be humane to animals; that it is permissible to kill them for food, but not to cause them undue suffering. "For man is a creature of chance and the beasts are creatures of chance, and one mischance awaits them all: death comes to both alike. They all draw from the same breath. Men have no advantage over beasts, for everything is emptiness. All go to the same place: all came from the dust, and to the dust all return" (Ecclesiastes 3:19).

Rabbi Abraham Isaac Kook, the first chief of pre-state Israel and one of the most important Jewish thinkers of the twentieth century, believed that a merciful God would not create a law permitting the killing of animals for food. Many Jews today base their vegetarianism on his beliefs, and vegetarianism among Jews—especially reconstructionist Jews—seems to be more prevalent than it is in the general population.

Christianity

Among Christian religions, only the Seventh-Day Adventists have strong views about the treatment of animals. Many Seventh-Day Adventists are vegetarians.

Christian doctrine has held that we have no obligations toward animals whatsoever. Saint Thomas Aquinas believed that killing animals was justified because they were put on this earth for our use. He believed it was okay for "more perfect" beings (humans) to kill for food. We don't need to extend our charity toward animals because they cannot "possess good," and because we have no fellow feeling with them. He believed that the only reason against cruelty to animals is that it may lead to cruelty to humans.

Even today, following the writings of Augustine and Aquinas, the Catholic Church maintains that we have no obligations toward animals. In 1988, however, Pope John Paul II issued a statement that represented some softening of this position: He urged "respect for the beings which constitute the natural world. . . . The dominion [power] granted to man by the Creator is not an absolute power, nor can one speak of a freedom to 'use and misuse,' to dispose of things as one pleases. . . . When it comes to the natural world, we are subject not only to biological laws, but also to moral ones, which cannot be violated with impunity [exemption from punishment]."

If you dig back far enough in the Christian tradition you can find some other examples of sympathy for animals. For one thing, the Messianic prophecies envisioned a world in which all creatures are at peace with one another. For another, the earliest Jewish Christians were vegetarians, and it is quite likely that vegetarianism was central to Christian beliefs immediately after the death of Jesus. Some historians argue, in fact, that it is likely that Jesus was a vegetarian.

ANIMAL RIGHTS: ANIMAL TESTING

In their behavior toward creatures, all men are Nazis.
—Isaac Bashevis Singer

If your interest in vegetarianism involves the ethical treatment of animals, you should learn how animals are used in scientific research and product tests, even if you feel squeamish about it. The mistreatment of animals forces us to ask the same ethical question: do the benefits (to humans) outweigh the drawbacks?

Terrible things are done to beagles, cats, rats, mice, and monkeys in the name of safety or science. Countless animals each year are shocked, poisoned, put in isolation from birth to make them severely depressed, put in decompression chambers, and forced to endure extreme heat—all to test the effects of this condition. Often these animals suffer needlessly, are not given anesthetic, and are not treated for injuries caused by the experiments.

The fact is that much of this animal testing is not necessary. Cosmetic and product tests on animals are not required by law. The Food and Drug Administration requires only that each ingredient used in a cosmetic be "adequately substantiated for safety." There

54

are many ways to substantiate safety; animal testing is not the only one. Yet every year thousands of animals are subjected to cruel and inhumane experiments in which poison is dropped into their eyes, and lethal doses of chemicals are given to see how long it takes them to die. Non-animal testing methods are just as reliable and are less expensive. Plus, manufacturers can make products using the many ingredients already determined safe by the Cosmetic or Fragrance Council.

In 1988 in Britain, 588,997 scientific procedures were performed on animals to test drugs and other materials. Of these procedures, nearly half were not related to the testing of medical or veterinary products. Worldwide it is estimated that nearly 14 million animals (including rats and mice) are involved each year in experiments that have nothing to do with testing medical products. In other words, animals are suffering and dying to test cosmetics and floor wax.

An American Medical Association representative testified before the United States Congress in hearings on drug testing that "frequently animal studies prove little or nothing and are very difficult to correlate to humans." Can humans benefit from tests on animals? Peter Singer says that the question is moot. Either the animal is not like us, in which case the tests do not correspond well with human conditions, so there is no reason to perform the experiment; or the animal is like us, in which case, how can we justify forcing an animal into an experiment that we would be horrified at if it were performed on a human?

six

STOP FACTORY FARMING

IF YOU WERE TO TAKE A DRIVE ON A BACK ROAD IN THE Midwest, you'd probably pass fields of corn and soybeans and see cows happily munching grass on gently rolling pastures. Or you might see them lolling under the shade of a tree, or drinking from

 a creek. Not a bad life for a cow, you think.

Unfortunately, what you are seeing is the exception, not the norm. Though cows spend more time outside than most animals raised for food, 90 percent of livestock are raised in some sort of confinement today. That means they are put in crowded, filthy pens and cages, often deprived of natural light, separated from their babies, and shot full of drugs and hormones that may be unhealthy to humans.

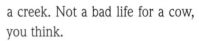

The way most people get their meat today—wrapped in plastic at the grocery store, cut up beyond recognition—allows them not to think too much about the fact that they're eating an animal, or about how that animal was raised for slaughter. Even using the words "beef" and "pork" removes us a step from the cows and pigs from which the meat comes.

Some people argue that it is natural for humans to eat animals and animal products. But is the way animals are raised today the slightest bit natural? The fact is, most people prefer not to think about where their food comes from.

Around the 1960s, as the demand for meat increased in the United States and in other countries, farmers began looking for more efficient—and more profitable—ways to raise animals for slaughter. Their methods have evolved into a system called factory farming.

Factory farming is so named because animals are treated as if they were products on a conveyor belt instead of living, breathing beings that feel pain and have emotions. Caring and feeding of the animals—tasks once performed by farmers—are now performed by machines. The result is mistreated animals, unhealthy conditions that promote stress and disease, and the increased use of hormones and other drugs to boost production.

People who believe in the humane treatment of animals aren't the only ones concerned about the big business of factory farming. Agricultural researchers and some farmers also protest the conditions in which these animals live. One farmer, interviewed by John Robbins for his book *Diet for a New America,* broke down in tears over the condition of his animals, saying he did not know what else to do. He and his family depended on the farm. Agribusiness concerns make it profitable and easy to go along with the system, and hard for those who don't.

The conditions for raising animals in this system are rivaled only by the inhumane conditions at the slaughterhouse. The source for most of this information is the farming industry itself. Many farmers today are horrified by the treatment of animals but feel powerless to stop the trend of factory farming. Others are now developing ways to raise lambs and rabbits in factory systems.

LAYING HENS

Used to be, a chicken was a chicken. But that was long before health-conscious Americans decided that "white meat" (chicken breasts) was healthier than red meat and began demanding it more than ever before. Today, chickens are bred either as "layers" (for eggs) or "broilers" (for meat).

In the United States, at least 95 percent of all eggs come from caged birds in automated factory buildings. Since males don't lay eggs and their flesh is of poor quality for eating, they are weeded out at the hatchery. Male chicks are typically thrown into heavy plastic bags, where they suffocate. The egg industry kills about half of its birds every year.

The ones that make it—the females—don't fare much better. The hens are crowded into cages so small that they cannot turn around or stretch their wings. The United Egg Producers in America recommended that each hen be given a mere 48 square inches (310 sq cm) of space—a bit less than the cover of this book. In fact, the hens were often allowed even less space.

Because their feathers constantly rub against the wire, some hens have few feathers, and the skin is rubbed raw. Because their claws were meant to scratch in dirt and not to rest on wire cages, their feet often get damaged. Their toenails can grow too long and get tangled up in the wire. The hens that get stuck in this way cannot reach their food or water, so they die. Rather than putting chickens back on a more natural surface, farmers solve this problem by cutting the hens' toes just beyond the nail.

BROILER CHICKENS

Under natural conditions, broiler chickens could expect to live about seven years. In factory farms, however, they are killed when they are about seven weeks old. During its short life, each chicken lives on a space that is smaller than a sheet of typing paper. The air the chickens breathe reeks of ammonia from their urine, and they often receive blisters and ulcers from standing and sitting on rotting, dirty litter. They never see the light of day or breathe fresh air. The crowded conditions make the chickens irritable and prone to fighting. They peck at each other's feathers and sometimes kill and eat one another.

To keep the birds' aggressions down, farmers keep the birds in near darkness. They also respond with other unnatural and cruel methods, such as debeaking, which means cutting off a bird's beak with a hot blade. This method, contrary to what some people say, is not a painless activity akin to cutting one's toenails. The beak has nerve endings and often bleeds after being cut. Some birds eat less and lose weight for several weeks after being debeaked.

Turkeys are raised under similar conditions. Instead of considering making the environment more natural, scientists are busy thinking up ways to genetically engineer a more docile bird that will not fight.

The United States lags far behind countries in Europe in remedying this horrific treatment of chickens. The minimum space allotment per chicken in Europe is 70 square inches (450 sq cm), almost twice the area required in the United States. In addition to this multinational recommendation, individual countries in Europe are acting to stop the abuse:

- In 1981, Switzerland began a ten-year phaseout of battery cages. In 1992, traditional cages were outlawed and all laying hens were provided with protected nesting boxes with a soft flooring.

- In the Netherlands, conventional cages were made illegal in 1994, and hens were given a minimum space allotment of about 150 square inches (970 sq cm) each, as well as access to scratching and nesting areas.
- Sweden passed a law in 1988 that called for the abolishment of cages for hens before 1998, and stated that cows, pigs, and animals raised for their furs must be kept "in as natural an environment as possible."

In the United States and other countries, you can purchase eggs from "free-range" hens, which basically means they are not caged. They may still, however, be confined to a large building. Check with a local natural foods store and then call the egg producer if you want to find out more.

PIGS

Factory farming of pigs has increased rapidly over the past few decades. By 1986, farms selling more than a thousand pigs a year produced more than 70 percent of the nation's supply. Ninety percent of pigs in the United States are in some type of confinement system. Two-thirds of them—some 53 million a year—spend their whole lives confined indoors, never seeing daylight until they are put on the truck to go to the slaughterhouse.

Inside the hog house, the floors are designed to be easy to clean and maintain; no thought is given to the comfort of the animal. The concrete or slatted floors damage the pigs' feet and legs. Some big operations stack hog cages on top of one another. The result is that excrement from the top pigs falls onto those below. The stench from the excrement also damages their lungs.

The pigs don't have straw to play with or other distractions, resulting in pigs that often turn neurotic and bite one another's tails. Instead of relieving the cause of this problem by changing the pigs' environment, farmers "dock" (cut) the pigs' tails without anesthetic.

DAIRY COWS

About half of the nation's ten million dairy cows and heifers (female cows who have not yet had a baby) are kept in some type of confinement system. In order to give milk, cows have to become pregnant every year. Their calves are taken from them at birth, a traumatizing experience for both. The mother often bellows incessantly for days after her calf is taken from her. The calf, denied its mother's milk, is fed a milk substitute for two years.

Many dairy cows are kept indoors in individual pens, with only enough room to stand up and lie down. Most milking operations are automated, and machines also feed the cows. Even the light, which affects milk production, is artificially set to get the most milk out of the cow. The cows are milked several times a day, causing their teats to become sore and often infected. When a cow has stopped producing milk, she goes to slaughter.

VEAL CALVES

Even many people who are not vegetarians refuse to eat veal because of the inhumane way calves are raised. Veal calves suffer the worst confinement of all animals raised for meat. Newborns are taken from their mothers immediately and placed in small stalls— about 22 inches wide and 54 inches long (56 x 135 cm)—that do not allow them to move around. Farmers don't want the calves to exercise, because those that develop muscle produce less tender meat. They are deliberately kept anemic—that is, denied any form of iron—so that their flesh will be white. Calves lick and chew iron bars and chains in a desperate attempt to get iron. They live in darkness to help keep them quiet. Calves are slaughtered at around four months. They wouldn't live much longer anyway because of their iron-deficient diet.

BEEF CATTLE

Compared to most other animals, beef cattle seem to have it easy. Many spend years grazing in open pasture. But most cattle—70 percent in the United States—still spend some time at a large feedlot, where they are fattened up before they are slaughtered. Some cattle spend all their lives on large feedlots, which now produce about a third of the nation's beef.

Beef cattle on feedlots are less restricted than most animals in factory operations, but they suffer in other ways. Nearly all farmers dehorn, brand or tag, and castrate their animals. Cows suffer when their horns are cut; the horns are not insensitive like fingernails but contain arteries and other tissue. Animals are castrated to make them more docile and easier to handle. Farmers do not use anesthesia for any of these procedures.

AT THE SLAUGHTERHOUSE

Life for these animals is no picnic, but the way they die is even more horrible. The ordeal begins with transportation to the slaughterhouse. Cows and pigs are crowded onto trucks; many go for days without food or water, and some are injured by shifting loads as they fall on top of one another. In recent years laws have been passed to require the watering and feeding of animals if they are kept on a truck for more than a couple of days.

At the slaughterhouse, the animals are kept in holding pens, waiting their turn to be killed. They can smell blood, hear the screams of their fellow animals, and sometimes even see what awaits them. In the United States, the Federal Humane Slaughter Act, passed in 1958, calls for the animal to be stunned unconscious before it is killed. In many cases this means a cow is literally clubbed over the head with a heavy sledgehammer to knock it out. If this doesn't work on the first try, it is clubbed again. In other cases, an animal is shot in the head with a stun gun to render it unconscious. Then the cow is shackled to the ceiling by one leg; its throat is slit and it is left to bleed to death.

But even the Humane Slaughter Act, inadequate as it is, has its limitations. It only applies to slaughterhouses that sell meat to the United States government or its agencies. Also, it does not apply to chickens or turkeys, which make up the largest number of animals killed. What's more, cows slaughtered in kosher meat-packing plants are exempt from the Humane Slaughter Act. They are not even rendered unconscious prior to slaughter. Because kosher law calls for not killing animals if they are injured, and stunning them or clubbing them is considered an injury, the cows are killed while fully conscious. Many countries, including the United States and Britain, allow an exception for slaughter according to Jewish and Muslim rules. Practically speaking, this means that the fully conscious cow is shackled by an ankle and hung in the air, often for five or ten minutes (longer if something goes wrong on the line), and the leg often breaks. After it has been strung up, its throat is slit. All the while it smells the blood of other animals whose throats have been slit.

Pretty hard stuff to stomach. That's about the worst of it, learning about the processes that bring meat to your table. But all these ethical, religious, and moral questions have so far dealt with just about everyone and everything but you. So let's now take a closer look at the direct benefits to you of a vegetarian diet.

seven

SAVE YOUR HEALTH

THE MESSAGE IS LOUD AND CLEAR. DOCTORS, RE-searchers, and nutritionists say vegetarianism is not only a safe, sound diet, it is actually healthier than meat-based diets. Vegetarianism does not require extensive planning, combining of foods to get complementary proteins in the same meal, or painstaking counting of protein grams. What's more, a vegetarian diet is perfectly safe for growing teenagers.

The American Heart Association, The American Cancer Society, the National Academy of Sciences, the American Academy of Pediatrics, and the American Dietetic Association have all urged Americans to reduce their consumption of animal fat and cholesterol and shift toward a diet that emphasizes grains, beans, fruits, and vegetables. That's just the sort of food a vegetarian diet consists of. (And make no mistake: fat usually comes from animals. More than

PRESCRIPTION:

TAKE 1 DAILY:

- Dr. Tant

Rx

half the fat in the American diet comes from animal foods; about a third comes from red meat.)

A major study of diet, lifestyle, and health in China suggests that lowering the intake of fat to 15 percent of calories prevents most cancers, diabetes, and heart disease. Known as the China Project, the study is a joint effort of Chinese, British, and American institutions. It tracked the diets of thousands of Chinese in dozens of countries. The results suggest that as fat consumption, protein consumption, and blood cholesterol levels rise, so does the incidence of heart disease, diabetes, and certain cancers.

But what about anemia or osteoporosis from deficiencies of iron or calcium? Wouldn't these conditions be more common if people aren't consuming meat and dairy products? In fact, no. Chinese villagers on low-fat diets who consume little meat also suffered less anemia and osteoporosis than urban Chinese who ate more meat. T. Colin Campbell of Cornell University, a coleader of the China Project, explained recently, "We're basically a vegetarian species and should be eating a wide variety of plant foods and minimizing our intake of animal foods."

Still not convinced? The statistics tell the story:

- In beef-eating Western cultures, colon cancer is up to ten times more common than in non-beef-eating cultures of Asia and developing countries.
- Scientists are beginning to link breast cancer with fat consumption—particularly animal-fat consumption. One of the largest cancer studies ever conducted found that women who eat meat daily have nearly four times the risk of getting breast cancer than those who eat meat less than once a week. The study was conducted in the 1970s at the National Cancer Research Institute in Tokyo.
- Men who eat animal products every day develop fatal prostate cancer 3.6 times more often than vegetarian men.

- Ovarian cancer is twice as likely to develop in women on high-fat diets than in women on low-fat diets (which could be vegetarian diets).
- Osteoporosis, the weakening of bones, is most common in countries where animal products, including milk, are consumed in the largest quantities.
- Men who eat meat three times a day are three times as likely to die from a heart attack than men who eat no meat.
- One out of three Americans is obese, defined as more than 20 percent above ideal body weight. (Also defined as total body fat content of more than 25 to 30 percent of body weight for men and more than 30 to 35 percent for women.) Obesity can be a serious health hazard. Studies show that vegetarians generally weigh less and have less body fat than meat eaters.
- Vegetarians are at lesser risk for constipation and lung cancer. Evidence also suggests that the risks for hypertension, coronary disease, certain types of diabetes, and gallstones are lower for vegetarians.

Many of these problems may seem like "old people's diseases" that you don't have to worry about. But some chronic conditions, such as hardening of the arteries, can begin as early as age fifteen. Many health experts say that American children's arteries are the most clogged of any in the world. Obesity is also a problem that often starts in adolescence. The American Heart Association reports that in a recent seventeen-year period, obesity in children aged six to eleven jumped 54 percent, and obesity in youths aged twelve to seventeen rose 39 percent. More children are overweight in America than ever before.

Researchers have learned recently how a meat-centered diet contributes to particular diseases and ailments. At the same time, they consistently see that a diet based on grains, fruits, and vegetables can make a person healthier. The bottom line: when people base their diets on meat, they are less likely to eat enough of good things such as fruits, vegetables, and whole grains and more likely to consume fat and cholesterol, which contribute to many diseases. The common thread running through the following information is that these diseases are rare or nonexistent in countries where the people do not consume high-fat, meat-based diets.

CANCER

Why do vegetarians have the edge against cancer? Environment and heredity are two big reasons people get cancer, but the National Cancer Institute says two out of three types of cancers are related to diet.

No one is exactly sure why a vegetarian diet seems to prevent cancer, but there are some clues. A team of German researchers, who have conducted an ongoing study of vegetarian males since 1978, have found that vegetarians have a much stronger immune system. Why? Because good vegetarian diets are lower in fat than most meat-based diets and heavy on vitamin-packed vegetables. Yellow and dark-green vegetables have a lot of beta-carotene, which may help boost your immune system. And many fruits and vegetables contain vitamin C, another immune-system booster. When your immune system is strong, it can fight off many types of cancer and other diseases.

What's more, toxins are held in fat tissue. So when you eat a piece of meat, you're eating the toxins that have been stored in the fat of the animal. Toxins are held in your body fat, too, so a low-fat vegetarian diet can help reduce the risk of these toxins causing cancer. Veggie diets are also typically high in fiber, which can help prevent colon cancer, because bad stuff is pushed out of your system before it can form cancer in your colon.

What other sorts of cancers can a vegetarian diet help prevent? Studies suggest that people who eat diets high in meat and dairy products and low in fiber are more likely to get colon cancer, breast cancer, uterine cancer, and prostate cancer. *Science,* the journal of the American Association for the Advancement of Science, concluded that "Populations on a high-meat, high-fat diet are more likely to develop colon cancer than individuals on vegetarian or similar low-meat diets." A study of Seventh-Day Adventists showed that rates of cancer for this largely vegetarian population were half that of meat eaters. Breast cancer is much less common among women in countries where low-fat vegetarian diets are the norm.

HEART DISEASE

What's heart disease got to do with you? Well, doctors have discovered that signs of heart disease can be found in people as young as fifteen.

Heart disease is the leading cause of death in the United States. But it wasn't always that way. Years ago, people generally ate a more balanced diet that included more fresh fruit, grains, and vegetables. Heart attacks were most common among the wealthy—those rich enough to afford a diet with a lot of meat, cheese, and cream. All of these foods contain a lot of cholesterol, the main culprit in heart disease. Cholesterol is a white, crystalline substance found in animal tissues and other foods. It's manufactured in the liver, and too much (especially the "bad" kind) can cause plaque to build up on the heart's arteries, restricting the flow of blood to the heart. Cholesterol also can cause arteries to close completely, leading to heart attacks.

Recent studies show that vegetarians have a much lower chance of developing heart disease than meat eaters. One study showed that men who ate meat every day (yes, that includes supposedly "low-fat" chicken) had three times the risk of dying from a heart attack as did vegetarian men. Another showed that lacto-ovo vegetarians have a 24 percent lower chance of developing heart disease; vegans, who eat no animal products, have a 57 percent lower risk of getting it. In general, vegetarians have lower cholesterol levels and blood-pressure rates than nonvegetarians.

OBESITY

Americans are too fat. And being too fat contributes to heart disease, hypertension (high blood pressure), liver disorders, gallbladder disease, cancer, arthritis, and other diseases. Studies show that vegetarians weigh less than meat eaters, and that pure vegetarians weigh even less and have far less body fat than meat eaters. Why? Because in general, vegetarians eat less fatty, calorie-dense foods and more fiber-rich, low-calorie foods. And as described in the cancer discussion above, cancer-causing toxins are stored in body fat.

ARTHRITIS

The Arthritis Foundation in the United States has not said outright that there may be a connection between diet and arthritis. In fact, most of this institution's research money goes toward testing drugs instead of researching the connection between diet and the disease. But it has to be more than coincidence that the highest rates of arthritis are found in countries where diets are based on meat and dairy products. In fact, in countries where the typical diet is low in fat and cholesterol, arthritis is almost unheard-of. At least a few researchers in the United States and Britain have found that when arthritis sufferers give up fats (meat and dairy products), their symptoms disappear.

OSTEOPOROSIS

There's a big debate over the main causes of osteoporosis. We know that heredity, drinking lots of soft drinks, not getting enough exer-

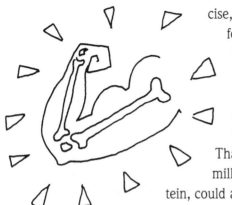

cise, and eating too much salt and junk food all contribute to bone fragility. But what's not as widely known is that too much protein—found in high concentrations in meat and animal products—can cause calcium loss and lead to osteoporosis. That means that drinking too much milk, which contains calcium and protein, could actually lead to calcium loss. In effect, the protein cancels out the calcium.

More than one hundred studies have demonstrated this phenomenon. Even so, the dairy industry continues to deny it. World Health Organization statistics show that osteoporosis is most common in the United States, Finland, Sweden, Israel, and the United Kingdom—where animal products are consumed in large quantities. What's more, though native Eskimo people have one of the highest rates of calcium intake in the world (some 200 milligrams a day, largely from fish bones) they also have one of the highest rates of osteoporosis in the world. Why? Some researchers believe it's because they have a very high protein intake (250 to 400 grams a day).

How does protein intake affect calcium stores in the body? Animal protein creates an acidic condition in the body. The body attempts to restore balance by taking calcium, an alkaline mineral, from the bones. So the more protein you consume, the more calcium is leached from your bones. The average American consumes twice the amount of protein recommended by the United Nations' Food and Agriculture Organization.

CAN WE TALK? CONSTIPATION AND OTHER DELICATE SUBJECTS

It's like this: our digestive systems were not designed to handle a lot of fat. Our intestines are long and curved, with many nooks and

70

crannies. They need a lot of roughage or fiber to keep things moving and to get rid of toxins. But when a diet is largely fat and little fiber, old fecal matter simply sits rotting away in your intestines, causing all sorts of problems. Not a pretty thought.

Many people with constipation problems take laxatives, which cause further problems because they harm intestinal walls. People may also develop a "spastic colon," a condition that is characterized by pain in the lower abdomen and alternating constipation and diarrhea. A high-fat diet often contributes to or even causes this condition. Appendicitis, too, is often caused by a small piece of hard, dry feces blocking the opening to the appendix.

VEGETARIAN DIETS AND TEENAGERS

Kids grow a lot—and fast—between the ages of twelve and twenty. So teenagers have different nutritional needs than adults. But since well-balanced vegetarian diets are nutritious, low in fat, and high in fiber, they are as good for teenagers as they are for older people. A 1994 article in the *American Journal of Clinical Nutrition* stated: "There is no doubt that a properly selected vegetarian diet can meet all the requirements of growing children, yet many health professionals still remain concerned about the adequacy of vegetarian diets."

If you plan it carefully, even a strict vegan diet provides all the nutrition you need. It's even easier for lacto-ovo vegetarians, the majority of vegetarians in most countries. What doctors worry about most in vegetarian diets is iron-deficiency anemia and vitamin B_{12} deficiency. But again, if you pay attention to the food you eat you can easily avoid these pitfalls. (See chapter ten, "A Crash Course in Nutrition.")

You may have heard that vegetarian children don't grow as tall or as fast as other kids, but that's just not true. It is true that children who have been raised on vegan or macrobiotic diets from birth grow more slowly in the first five years of their life, but they catch up by age ten. And these are vegan and macrobiotic diets, not a less restrictive lacto-ovo diet. But many people hear about these studies and generalize that vegetarian diets aren't good for growing teens. In fact, many studies (including a large, long-term study of Seventh-Day Adventist children) have shown that vegetarian children grow as tall and as big as meat-eating children and that they grow at a healthy rate. A study of more than four hundred vegan children in Tennessee showed that kids can grow tall and strong even when they don't eat dairy products or eggs.

Other studies have shown that adolescent girls on a vegetarian diet begin their menstrual periods later than other girls. But that's not a bad thing. The delayed onset of menstruation has been associated with a decreased incidence of several kinds of cancer, particularly breast cancer, later in life.

SAFER FOOD

If you're a vegetarian, there's another bonus: the food you eat tends to be less prone to disease and contamination. Though there is continuing concern about pesticides on vegetables and fruits, a 1988 Canadian study found more residues of pesticides on eggs and meat. That's probably because most pesticides are fat-soluble, so high-fat foods (eggs, cheese, meat) tend to have higher levels of contamination than low-fat foods (fruits and vegetables).

Most of the contamination of meat is a result of lax inspection standards. The chicken industry, for example, is so bad that even the inspectors are disgusted. Sixty of the eighty-four poultry inspectors interviewed by John Robbins in his book *May All Be Fed* said that they no longer eat chicken. Inspectors are pressured not to have too many "bad" birds on their tally. They are harassed by their supervisors and by company officials. A USDA (United States Department of Agriculture) microbiologist in Athens, Georgia, tested precooked "ready to eat" store-bought chickens and found that 98 percent of them were contaminated. One inspector told Robbins,

"I'm ashamed to even let people know I am a USDA inspector. There are thousands of diseased and unwholesome birds going right on down the lines."

Salmonella poisoning, a bacterial infection that people get from eating contaminated animal products, makes thousands of people sick every year and causes dozens of deaths. It is a form of food poisoning that causes intestinal discomfort, vomiting, chills, fever, and headaches. In most cases these symptoms begin within a day of eating contaminated food and last up to a week. For people in high-risk groups, however, such as infants and the elderly, the disease can be fatal. And it is on the rise in the United States. The number of cases has doubled in the past sixteen years or so. It used to occur in eggs that were cracked or contaminated by chicken droppings, but now it appears that even intact, sanitized eggs can contain it. That is, the bacteria can be transmitted to an egg even while it is inside the hen's ovaries.

Scientists and the general public have been paying attention to slaughterhouse conditions ever since the publication of *The Jungle,* by Upton Sinclair, in 1906. In this ground breaking book, Sinclair exposed the unsanitary conditions in the slaughterhouses of Chicago. He used such graphic detail to describe what he saw that readers sent up an immediate uproar. Two years later, the United States passed the Pure Food and Drug Act, and also a Meat Inspection Act. But such responses to the public outcry have not eliminated all unsanitary conditions.

Regulations for meat inspection have changed in recent years to allow meat packers and inspectors to work more quickly. In the early 1990s, the USDA and several of the giant meat packers began using a new inspection process called the Streamlined Inspection System (SIS) that basically eliminates the role of the federal meat inspector in examining beef carcasses. SIS was intended to make the industry self-regulating and rely on random spot checks to detect problems. The trouble is, every cow is unique—cows are not machine parts that come off an assembly line. That means that because federal inspectors no longer inspect each carcass for disease, some diseased animals are quite likely making their way to your supermarket.

Inspection standards have been relaxed. The new justification is that beef doesn't need to be free of all contaminants. Many federal meat inspectors have spoken out strongly against this new system and are calling for new regulations. A joint letter sent in the early 1990s by twenty-four inspectors to the National Academy of Sciences states: "In good conscience, we can no longer say that we know USDA approved beef is wholesome. . . . USDA advertises the SIS as fewer inspectors looking at less meat on more carcasses at faster line speeds, all without lowering public health standards. We don't buy it." What's more, scientists are discovering new cattle diseases every day—diseases that are not being monitored at all.

In response to all the criticism, the USDA announced a plan in early 1995 to require processing plants to conduct daily tests for contamination with salmonella bacteria. Details are still being hashed out, and the industry will be allowed up to three years to implement whatever changes are required.

Another concern about meat quality is that people who eat meat are affected by the antibiotics that those animals consume. Farmers put small amounts of common antibiotics such as penicillin and tetracycline into the livestock's feed to help them grow and discourage disease. But these antibiotics are then consumed by the people who eat their flesh. Many scientists believe that these people then develop bacteria that are resistant to common antibiotics. The use of antibiotics has increased a whopping 400 percent over the past twenty years as farmers try to get more weight out of their livestock.

As if all that weren't enough to put you off meat forever, cattle in Britain are falling prey to a "mad-cow disease" that many scientists are afraid can be transmitted to humans. The disease, called bovine spongiform encephalopathy, attacks cows' brains, making them spongelike. The cows are driven crazy and then they die. No one is quite sure how cows get the disease, but the theory is that it came from a brain disease in sheep called scrapie. For years cows were fed the ground-up bone and meat remnants—including brains—of sheep.

Also unclear is whether humans can get sick from eating a cow with mad-cow disease. Many people are worried there could be a link between the bovine disease and Creutzfeldt-Jakob disease, a rare brain disease that's fatal to humans. Both diseases have the same pathology, or basic characteristics. Scientists have not established a direct link between the two, but the British government has announced that there is a possible link between the human disease and eating beef infected with the disease.

Scientists are investigating the deaths of eight people in England who suffered from Creutzfeldt-Jakob disease. All eight were known to eat beef or dairy products. In any case, Britons and other Europeans who eat British beef have become very worried at the possibility of a link, so millions of cows are being destroyed as a safeguard. What's more, one in four Britons say they no longer eat red meat.

Fish, by the way, don't come out swimmingly either in the food safety analysis. Nearly half of the fish tested by *Consumer Reports* magazine in a six-month investigation were contaminated by bacteria (from human or animal feces), and some fish were contaminated with PCBs and mercury. The Centers for Disease Control in Atlanta, Georgia, report that fish account for about 10 percent of gastrointestinal illnesses in America. Most seafood-related illnesses are from raw shellfish harvested in waters contaminated with raw or poorly treated sewage. The inspection system for seafood in the United States is hit-and-miss and in desperate need of overhauling, experts say.

eight

SAVE THE CHILDREN:
CAN THE WORLD AFFORD A MEAT HABIT?

"The transfer of the world's grain production from food to feed is among the most significant changes in the redistribution of wealth in the whole of recorded history."
—Jeremy Rifkin, *Beyond Beef*

CHRONIC HUNGER AFFECTS MORE THAN 1.3 BILLION people in the world, according to the World Health Organization. That's nearly 30 percent of the world population. Never before in human history has such a large percentage of people been without adequate food.

Why? People like to blame overpopulation. They point out that the world's resources simply cannot support all the people on the planet. But the fact is that the world could support all its people on a plant-based diet; it just can't support a whole world full of people who center their diets around meat. Neither overpopulation nor underproduction is the basic cause of hunger in the world. In Ireland's great potato famine in the nineteenth century, for example, the problem was not a lack of food (Ireland was exporting wheat at the same time its people were starving to death) but rather the lack of access to that food.

More recently, all of the poor countries south of the Sahara Desert in Africa have been affected by widespread famine. These countries, in what is called the Sahel, have produced enough grain to feed all their people, even during the worst years of drought in the early 1970s. A number of these countries actually increased their exports of cotton, peanuts, and vegetables at a time when their people were starving. What's important is not just increasing food production or decreasing world population but redistributing available food more fairly.

Unfortunately, while interest in vegetarianism or non-meat-based diets is growing among certain societies, meat eating still means status in developing countries, and the demand for meat continues to increase. United States agricultural interests are exporting a "meat culture" to developing countries. In those countries, the demand for meat among the rich is squeezing out the production of staple foods—grains and beans—that could feed the poor.

Consider these facts from the North American Vegetarian Society:

- 1.3 billion people could be fed with the grain and soybeans eaten by U.S. livestock. The U.S. population is only 255 million.
- 80 percent of U.S. corn and 95 percent of U.S. oats are eaten by livestock.
- 90 percent of protein, 99 percent of carbohydrates, and 100 percent of dietary fiber is wasted by cycling grain through animals.
- 64 percent of American agricultural land is used to grow feed for livestock.
- An acre (.4 ha) of land can yield 250

pounds (114 kg) of beef or 40,000 pounds (18,000 kg) of potatoes.

- It takes 16 pounds (7 kg) of grain and soybeans to produce 1 pound (.45 kg) of beef.
- Fifteen vegetarians can be fed on the same amount of land needed to feed one person on a meat-based diet.

And, according to a recent World Watch Institute Report:

- 73 percent of imports from developing nations of corn, barley, sorghum, and oats are fed to animals, not people.

Most of the nations that now import grain from the United States were once self-sufficient in grain. The reason they import grain is not to feed more people but to feed cows and pigs to satisfy a growing demand for meat among the wealthiest members of these societies.

In Taiwan, for example, the per-capita consumption of meat and eggs increased sixfold between 1950 and 1990. With the rise in meat and egg consumption came a rise in grain consumption: from 375 pounds to 858 pounds (170 kg to 389 kg) per person per year during those forty years. In 1950 Taiwan was a grain exporter. By 1990 the nation imported, mostly for animal feed, 74 percent of the grain it used.

Taiwan is hardly alone. In mainland China, meat consumption has doubled since 1978. Chinese farmers have been able to grow enough feed to keep up with the needs of the growing meat industry so far, but few experts expect that they will be able to keep pace much longer. The share of Chinese grain fed to livestock rose from 7 percent in 1960 to 20 percent in 1990.

Just twenty years ago, Egypt was self-sufficient in grain production. Its livestock ate only 10 percent of the grain it produced. Today livestock eat 36 percent, and Egypt is forced to import 8 million tons of grain per year.

Even in the former Soviet Union an increase in meat consumption has severely worsened the area's already complicated economic and social ills. Since 1950, meat consumption there has tripled and grain consumption has quadrupled. Today, Russian livestock eat three times more grain than Russian citizens. In 1970, the Soviet Union imported hardly any grain, but by 1990 that area imported 24 million tons. Not only is it an economic burden, sometimes a disaster, for a country to have to import such a basic product, but the implications of being heavily dependent on imports reach far beyond the simple monetary cost.

Throughout developing nations, the production of meat is devastating the natural ecosystem, monopolizing the best local land, undermining the local food supply, and undercutting efforts of the people to be self-sufficient.

The situation in Latin America is particularly complicated. International lending agencies feed billions of dollars in loans to the livestock industry. But more than half of Latin America's beef is exported, and what's left is too expensive for any but the very wealthy to buy. In 1987, the United States imported 150,000 tons of meat from Central and South America.

In Brazil, black beans used to be a cheap source of protein for the poor. But when farmers began to realize that they could get more money for growing animal feed crops, they stopped growing black beans. Now even black beans are a more expensive product as a result. So market forces can influence other seemingly stable elements of a country's economy.

While a typical acre of land in Latin America can easily produce more than 1,200 pounds (540 kg) of grain per year, that same land used to graze cattle barely yields 50 pounds (23 kg) of meat. Farmers turn increasingly to less efficient but more profitable meat production. Also, since 1960 the number of landless people in Central America has multiplied fourfold, and the trend toward land consolidation can be traced directly to the production of meat.

Let's imagine for a moment that you and everyone else in the world have given up eating meat. Some experts believe that if the whole world were to turn vegetarian tomorrow, there would be enough food to go around for all humans. Does this mean there would be an end to world hunger? Unfortunately, no. Meat production is not directly responsible for hunger in the world. Most of the world's starving people are so poor that they cannot afford to buy food—any food.

Even in a world full of vegetarians—but especially in our real world of competing interests—feed grain (oats, corn, and wheat that are grown to feed livestock) could be needed to fight hunger in the future. World grain production per capita has been declining since 1984. If this trend continues, we'll need feed grains to feed hungry people.

But food is a complicated issue, involving politics, social mores, and economics. If the demand for meat suddenly disappeared, there's no guarantee that farmers in poor countries would then begin growing food to feed their own people. Vegetarians cannot set social policy. But it is easy to see why some people feel uncomfortable eating beef imported from a poor Latin American country where many people cannot afford to buy food for themselves.

In 1974, Lester Brown of the Overseas Development Council estimated that if Americans were to reduce their meat consumption by only 10 percent for one year—or to put it another way, if 10 percent of Americans turned vegetarian—at least 12 million tons of grain could be freed up for human consumption. That would be enough grain to feed 60 million people. Again, if demand for meat went down, there's no guarantee that farmers would return to growing crops for human consumption, but that's the hope.

THE FUTURE

How will we feed future generations when we are losing cropland and gaining population? Estimates are that the world's population will almost double in the next fifty years. A few scientists, such as Dennis Avery, Director of Global Food Issues at the Hudson Institute in Indianapolis, believe that high-tech farming, free trade, and bio-engineering are the keys to tripling food production without plowing new fields or destroying wildlife habitats. Certainly farming could be more efficient, although many have argued that the major scientific breakthroughs in farming have already occurred. But no matter how you slice it, far less land is needed to grow crops for a plant-based diet.

Other scientists believe that it is inevitable that we will all become vegetarians in the years to come, like it or not. They believe that the world simply cannot sustain a meat-based diet and that the rest of us will join the three-quarters of the world's population that lives on—indeed, thrives on—a diet of grains, fruits, and vegetables. Of course, there's also the possibility that Westerners will refuse to adapt their diets and that wars will be fought over food.

Perhaps the question is, does it make sense to engineer new ways to produce food for the typical American meat-and-dairy diet for export to a growing world when this diet has been shown to cause obesity, heart disease, and cancer? And isn't there something to be said for cultural diversity, for preserving the traditional foods of many of the world's great cultures? What sort of world is it if everyone from Japan to Italy is eating burgers and fries?

nine

TAKE CONTROL OF WHAT YOU EAT

WHO CONTROLS WHAT YOU EAT? THIS MIGHT SOUND like an absurd question. But food habits are ingrained in us from when we are very young, and they come from a variety of sources. Our parents, of course, shape a lot of our attitudes about food. We are also born with various taste preferences, some of which may change over the years. Cultural and societal customs play a big role.

The Chinese, for instance, would not think of having a meal without rice or noodles. Muslims do not eat pork, considering it a dirty animal. Hindus don't eat cows, which they consider sacred.

In the United States, Britain, and many other western countries, a "good" meal has for years been centered around a large piece of meat, with potatoes and some vegetables on the side. The reasons for such preferences are complicated. Some date back to the Great

Depression of the 1930s, when food was rationed and meat, milk, butter, and cheese were scarce. Many older people still equate beans and grains with poverty, and these associations are hard to dispel.

But another reason people in America and other countries consume so much meat and dairy products is the influence of the beef, pork, chicken, and dairy councils. These are, in fact, powerful industries that spend millions of dollars convincing the public their products are essential for good health. They fund scientific studies trying to "prove" the healthfulness of their products. They produce nutrition information and distribute it in the nation's schools. These industries also advertise in magazines and newspapers and on radio and television.

ADVERTISING

One of the biggest marketing lies of recent times has been the pork industry's claim that pork is the "other white meat." For one thing, of course, pork is not white meat. For another, the real white meat, chicken and turkey, is not a super health food. It contains a lot of fat and cholesterol, unlike vegetables, whole grains, fruits, beans, and dried peas.

The National Cattlemen's Beef Association routinely features a three-ounce steak in its ads to suggest that beef is low in fat. The average steak serving, though, is more like six ounces. A similar ad in the early 1990s for Frank Perdue, the chicken giant, listed the amount of fat for one ounce of roasted chicken. Sure, it looks pretty low, until you multiply it by five to get a typical serving size of five ounces.

The lesson? Read these ads with a grain of salt. Advertisers do not play by the same rules as do dietary agencies or physicians' groups.

INFILTRATING THE SCHOOLS

Advertising isn't the only way people receive information. There's school, too! Meat and dairy interests know that by presenting information to young schoolchildren in the classroom, they've got a good chance of appearing to be a credible source of information. This information shapes attitudes that stay with you years after you encounter them in grade school, maybe your whole life.

Perhaps you didn't know that industries with an economic interest in the information presented were allowed to distribute materials in schools. It is up to teachers and administrators, of course, to decide what they will present to students. But because many schools are underfunded these days, overworked teachers are happy to have free materials to use in the classroom. They seldom have the time or resources to investigate the claims made in these materials.

The National Dairy Council is one of the leading suppliers of materials used to teach nutritional education in American schools. Sometimes the message is subtle, sometimes blatant, but always the same: dairy products are good for you. A coloring book for young schoolchildren instructs students to use the color green for the face of a dad who does not drink his milk and pink for the dad who does. Another pamphlet tells children that ice cream is a "healthful food made from milk and cream along with other good foods." (Nowhere does it mention the fat and sugar in ice cream.) One handout advises children to "drink milk at every meal and have . . . cheese, ice cream, baked custard, [and a]

bowl of cream of tomato soup with butter." Talk about fat. A section on "low-calorie" nutrition suggests eating balls of cream cheese, softened with cream and rolled in chopped nuts. This snack is about 90 percent fat!

The Dairy Council is not the only one providing misleading information to kids in schools. A few years ago, McDonald's printed a sixteen-page ad that was later distributed to schools around Chicago, Illinois. "Good Food, Good Nutrition, and McDonald's" purported to discuss a properly balanced diet. Its example: a cheeseburger, fries, a chocolate shake, and McDonaldland cookies.

The Oscar Mayer Company also provides schools with free nutritional materials. The materials compare sausage products with such high-fat foods as margarine, mayonnaise, salad dressing, and cream cheese, and declare that their sausages aren't really all that fatty. Sausage also has less cholesterol than eggs, the materials point out, though they fail to mention that eggs have the most cholesterol of any food. And they tell us that hot dogs have less sugar and more nutrients than a 12-ounce can of cola. No kidding!

Some of these examples may be a few years old, and we have picked some of the worst to make our point. But you can see how attitudes about food are formed when such information is presented in schools. And things haven't gotten much better. In 1995 the Indiana Farm Bureau produced a video aimed at younger kids called "Where Pork Comes From." The film talks about how pork producers "care" about their animals, and how pork is "leaner today" and part of a "healthy, balanced diet." More recently, meat and dairy associations have been trying to clean up their image, making sure to mention skim milk, low-fat cheeses and yogurt, skinless chicken, and other "healthy" foods.

Meat and dairy industries are trying harder than ever to make sure their voice is heard. And they've got the money to do it. The Arizona Beef Council's literature cites a study conducted by the National Beef and Livestock Board which concludes that food shoppers who call themselves vegetarians "eat only slightly less meat than meat eaters." They want you to believe that we all love meat, even though some of us may be "in the closet" about it.

The lesson here? Know who's behind your sources of information.

LIFE IN THE CAFETERIA

It is bad enough that students get biased, outdated, and just plain bad nutrition information through their teachers. But when you go to the cafeteria, you're confronted with bad nutrition in a more immediate way. The United States Department of  Agriculture buys surplus food and donates it to the nation's schools. Such donations make up 20 to 30 percent of food in school lunches. This surplus program guarantees a market for the meat and dairy industry in order to keep prices stable. In all, the USDA provides between three and four billion dollars' worth of guaranteed business to the meat and dairy industries through its surplus program. In 1991, 90 percent of the USDA surplus consisted of eggs, high-fat cheeses, butter, ground pork, and ground beef.

Luckily, the dairy and meat industries are not the only ones providing nutritional information to schools. As the vegetarian movement grows and becomes stronger, several organizations are fighting back by providing their own information to students and are working to bring healthier lunches to schools. The Farm Animal Reform Movement (FARM) is developing a school lunch and education program, called "Choice," that will encourage students to explore healthy choices such as fruits, vegetables, and grains. The program is not in place yet, but Choice hopes to get volunteers in schools to talk about how a diet based on vegetables, grains, and fruits can make teens strong and alert. The organization EarthSave's Healthy School Lunch Program provides recipes to cafeteria food-service directors for nutritious, low-fat, vegetarian meals.

THE GOVERNMENT

Turns out that you even have to be skeptical of dietary information you get from your government, at least if you live in the United States and Canada. Remember the four basic food groups? The United States Agriculture Department and Department of Health and Human Services have a joint committee that adopts a set of recommendations called the Dietary Guidelines for Americans. They used to present those food groups in four equal-sized squares, with suggestions for the number of servings to eat from each group. Later, they changed the form to a food pyramid, to provide a better visual sense of how much to eat from each food group.

The Dietary Guidelines for Americans come up for review every five years. In the 1995 review, here's how the USDA Dietary Guidelines looked:

FOOD GUIDE PYRAMID
A Guide to Daily Food Choices

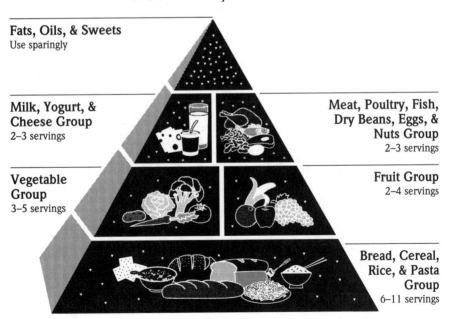

Fats, Oils, & Sweets
Use sparingly

Milk, Yogurt, &
Cheese Group
2–3 servings

Meat, Poultry, Fish,
Dry Beans, Eggs, &
Nuts Group
2–3 servings

Vegetable
Group
3–5 servings

Fruit Group
2–4 servings

Bread, Cereal,
Rice, & Pasta
Group
6–11 servings

While the guidelines were under review, a group of prominent physicians and heart researchers recommended what would seem to be a rather radical step: demote meat and dairy from two or three servings a day each to "optional." The recommendation to eat two to three servings of both meat and dairy per day flies in the face of medical research, says Andrew Nicholson, a member of the Physicians Committee for Responsible Medicine (PCRM), the group that recommended changes to the guidelines. Even a small amount of meat each day will push a person past the fat intake most doctors recommend (15 to 20 percent of total calories). The PCRM also called for the creation of a legume group to include beans, peas, and lentils (recommending two to four servings). The bottom line: Americans should replace meat and dairy with vegetables, fruits, legumes, and grains, not just supplement their diet with them.

The USDA did not change its basic pyramid to create a legume group and make meat and dairy optional. But it did, for the first time, endorse vegetarian diets as healthy. This endorsement was a big victory for PCRM and other vegetarian health activists. It is doubtful that the USDA would relegate meat and dairy to optional status, because the USDA is under tremendous pressure from powerful lobbies with vested interests in the guidelines. In addition, the USDA believes that Americans simply cannot change their eating habits so drastically. Many doctors believe it is "unrealistic" to ask people to give up meat and dairy products. But nutritionists and health activists today are asking why people are not being told about the best thing they can do to prevent many diseases: give up meat completely and cut way back on dairy products. It can be done: let's not forget that twenty-five years ago, many doctors believed it was "unrealistic" to ask their patients to quit smoking!

The situation is not much different in Canada. There, the government gave in to pressures from the meat and dairy industries to include more servings of meat and eggs in its revised Canada Food Guide, issued in 1993. In the early 1990s, Health and Welfare Canada, the Canadian equivalent of the United States Department of Agriculture, drafted a proposed Food Guide that called for less fat, in the form of meat, eggs, and dairy products. It called for one serving of meat, one egg, and two to four servings of milk each day. Each of these changes met with an uproar of disapproval from the industries that produce these products. In the end, the Canadian government changed its recommendations. Here is the food guide it came up with:

Grain Products	5 to 12 servings per day
Vegetables and Fruit	5 to 10 servings per day
Milk Products	2 to 3 (children 4 to 9 years)
	3 to 4 (youths 10 to 16 years)
	2 to 4 (adults)
	3 to 4 (pregnant and breast-feeding women)
Meat and Meat Alternatives (includes eggs)	2 to 3 servings per day

HOW GOING VEG. AFFECTS YOUR HEAD

Well, if you've read this far then you either were a vegetarian to begin with or you're thinking about becoming one now. Should you go gradually into the vegetarian world or become a vegetarian overnight? There's no right way. Some people find it easier to cut out meats gradually: first beef and pork, then chicken, then fish, then perhaps even eggs and dairy products.

If you give up meat overnight, you might find that you feel less energetic at first. That's not because vegetarian diets make people feel less energetic but because your body is adjusting to the radical change. Specifically, the mucous lining in your intestines may have to adjust to not processing all that fat, and if it hasn't, the magnesium and riboflavin from plant foods may have a harder time getting into the bloodstream. Your system should adjust in a couple of weeks. In fact, most vegetarians quickly report feeling better than ever.

One advantage to quitting all at once: some psychologists believe that small dietary changes are harder to stick with. They believe that if you cut down on meat gradually, you will still have a taste for it but will be frustrated because you're not eating much. Better to quit cold turkey (so to speak), and you will lose your taste for meat that much faster. There are only four basic tastes the tongue can detect—sweet, sour, salty, and bitter. Fat, though, is an acquired taste. So to lose the taste for it you can just cut it out. For instance, people who have switched to skim milk will tell you that whole milk now tastes too rich and thick for them. Don't despair if vegetables are not your favorite food. Many teens who make the switch to vegetarianism say that they gradually begin to develop a taste for different foods.

Socially, you may run into more criticism and comments from others on your new diet if you switch overnight. Gradually giving up animal products means that people are less apt to notice and question you about your food choices. How this affects you depends on how you feel about vegetarianism. Do you want it to be a political and social statement? Do you want people to know and engage you in discussions about your diet? Or would you rather it be a private matter? Your parents may think your vegetarianism is less "radical" if you slowly cut out meat. On the other hand, many teens report that once they've made the decision to stop eating meat, it's easier to do it all at once.

HOW GOING VEG. AFFECTS YOUR BODY

After you've stopped eating meat, you might find that you're hungry more often. This is because you no longer have that big hunk of meat sitting in your stomach taking a long time to digest. More technically, meat and animal products are dense with calories and fat, so they will stick with you longer than carbohydrates, such as pasta, bread, and rice. Again, in time your body will adjust, but you might want to make sure to have a stock of healthy snacks on hand—rice cakes, nuts, dried and fresh fruits, bagels, popcorn—to alleviate that empty feeling. Nutritionists (and weight-loss experts) recommend that people eat many small meals during the day instead of a few heavy ones, so this sort of eating is quite acceptable.

You might lose weight. That's because a vegetarian diet is rich in the foods—vegetables, grains, fruits—that take up a lot of bulk but do not add on the calories. That's great if you need to shed pounds. If you are lean already, though, make sure to get enough calories by filling up on such calorie-dense foods as beans, nuts, and nut butters.

And just so you know, you might gain weight. Plenty of champion athletes (like Dave Scott, six-time Ironman triathlon winner) and even some wrestlers (Killer Kowalski) have bulked up or retained their physiques on a vegetarian diet. The point is, you are taking control of your diet. So you can tailor your diet to fit your needs. If you're interested in gaining, losing, or staying the same, you can do it better without meat.

And just so you know this, too: flatulence (gas) can be an embarrassing problem for those adjusting to a new diet of fiber and legumes. To remedy the problem, make sure beans and dried peas are cooked thoroughly, and introduce them into your diet slowly, in small amounts, to give your body time to adjust. Start with the easier-to-digest legumes: split peas, lima beans, adzuki beans, mung beans, and lentils (generally, the smaller the bean or legume, the easier it is to digest). If you pre-soak beans or peas, make sure to drain the soaking water and cook in fresh water to help reduce the gas-producing effect. You can also try Beano or one of the other commercial products sold in drugstores and health food stores that help alleviate excess gas from beans and vegetables. If you're using canned beans, drain and rinse them before using.

HOW GOING VEG. AFFECTS YOUR SOCIAL LIFE

Unfortunately, you may be in for some teasing, mostly from friends but maybe from your own family, too. Most of it will be good-natured but it can be very annoying. Your friends and siblings might try to "tempt" you to eat meat by waving hamburgers under your nose. They may chide you for eating "rabbit food." Other people might get more unpleasant, challenging you if you wear leather shoes or constantly monitoring you to see if you "slip up." Some people  just can't imagine doing what you're doing, so they assume that everyone—even long-time vegetarians—secretly craves meat.

At Home Your parents may be downright angry about your decision, perhaps because they see it as a slap in the face to their way of life, because they are afraid for your health, or because they see it as a rebellion that will disrupt the home. As always, the best defense is knowledge. If you can convince your parents that you're eating better than ever, maybe you can really impress them rather than rub them the wrong way.

You face a major disadvantage compared to other vegetarians: you don't control the kitchen, either at home or at school. Many people stop eating meat when they leave home or go away to college. It's not impossible to become a vegetarian while still at home, however, if you have the right parents or can convince them to cooperate.

The first thing to do is arm yourself with information to present to them. You could hand them a copy of this book (pointing out especially the chapters on health and nutrition) or give them a shorter, more concise pamphlet to introduce them to vegetarianism. Write to the American Dietetic Association, the North American Vegetarian Association, or the Vegetarian Resource Group for some information (see chapter twelve, "Knowledge Is Power").

Once your parents are convinced that being a vegetarian will not harm your health, you may also need to convince them that your diet will not cause turmoil at meal times. Some parents may willingly cook a separate dinner for you; others won't be so accommodating. Others may be willing to alter basic recipes: you might suggest that they leave the meat out of half of the lasagna, off half the pizza, or (if you're eating eggs) out of the quiche. Suggest filling these dishes with spinach or other diced, cooked vegetables. They can fix the ingredients for tacos or burritos separately, and you can add refried beans (the vegetarian variety—made without lard—is easy to find these days) instead of taco meat. If they're making a soup, stew, or stir-fry, perhaps they'll add the meat at the end, after you've scooped out some for yourself (you might ask that they use a vegetable stock and that they throw in some cooked beans).

If, however, you get no such cooperation, you've got a few choices. One is, learn to cook. You only need to know a few basic recipes to get going. When a dish works well for you, you can offer to cook it and add it to the meal. Choose something that goes along with the family dinner—a ratatouille (Italian vegetable stew) or white bean salad to go with spaghetti and meatballs, or corn and black bean salsa or Spanish rice with green pepper, onion, zucchini, and tomato to complement a Mexican meal. If you've got some talent in the kitchen, you might convert your parents, or at least encourage them to cut back on meat.

Other things to make life easier at home? Offer to do some of the grocery shopping, and stock up on easy-to-prepare veggie foods. Ready-to-eat soups, frozen dinners, premade frozen veggie burgers, tofu dogs, dip mixes, and other convenience foods make for easy dinners. You can also learn to "eat around" your family's dinner, depending on what they're having. Eat a bigger portion of salad, and add some fresh spinach and canned chickpeas for a nutrition boost. Eat more bread (with luck, it'll be whole grain), and spread some tahini or peanut butter on it. Top your baked potato with soy cheese or low-fat cottage cheese. And don't forget about breakfast foods. A bowl of fortified cereal with dairy or soy milk and fruit is an acceptable meal nutritionally. Same goes for whole-grain pancakes topped with fruit.

But even if all goes well, and your parents tolerate your different eating habits, be prepared for continued skepticism. If you get a cold or infection, your parents might automatically blame it on your vegetarian diet. Although it's not true that vegetarians are more prone to sickness, all the medical studies in the world won't convince a parent who doesn't want to be convinced. In such a case, there is not much you can do but put up with it.

At School Unless your school cafeteria *actually* offers vegetarian entrées, the main dishes are things like burgers, meat tacos, sausage pizza, and hot ham-and-cheese sandwiches. What's a vegetarian student to do? Head for the salad bar, if your school has one. Ask for two servings of vegetables, and load up on the potatoes. Bring an instant cup-of-soup from home to round out your school meal. If the cafeteria has very limited options, you could brown-bag it altogether. Good things to tote to school: carrot and celery sticks, fruit, low-fat yogurt, vegetable-and-cheese sandwiches on whole-grain bread or buns, peanut butter and jelly sandwiches, or pita bread stuffed with hummus (a chickpea spread), tomato, and cucumber.

Fortunately, some groups are working to improve the school lunch situation. EarthSave's Healthy Lunch Program is working with teachers, principals, and food-service directors to teach them the benefits of low-fat, vegetarian lunches. The program operates in several schools across the country. And at colleges around the country, students are lobbying to get vegetarian and even vegan food in the dorm cafeterias. A group called Vegan Action in Berkeley, California, was recently successful in getting the residence hall cafeterias at the University of California to offer vegan food.

At a Friend's House   How you act as a vegetarian depends a lot on the type of person you are. Some vegetarians prefer not to make waves, so they eat around the food served at family dinners, eating the salad, bread, and side dishes, and perhaps even putting a small piece of meat on their plates without eating it. But that sort of compromising can get old after a while (plus, you may just start getting hungry!).

So what do you do when you're invited to dinner at the house of someone who doesn't know you're a vegetarian? You don't want to make the host uncomfortable, but you also don't feel like apologizing for being a vegetarian. Again, you can handle it in different ways. Perhaps you don't want to volunteer the information unless you're asked. In fact, a gracious and perceptive host will ask about their guests' food preferences. He or she might say, "I'm serving fish; is that OK?" If it's not OK with you, this is the time to speak up. They wouldn't have asked if they didn't really want to know.

If the host does ask about your food preferences, do not feel as though you need to apologize. You could just say, "Oh, I don't eat fish or other types of meat, but I'm sure there will be plenty more for me to eat." Or "I'm sure I can find enough food to eat." In some situations you can also offer to bring a vegetarian dish. Barbecues and potlucks are easier than sit-down dinners; you can always bring some tofu dogs or veggie burgers to throw on the grill.

What if the host doesn't ask? Again, it depends on your personality, and perhaps on the situation. If you're all right finding enough to eat without touching the main course, that's fine. Even then, though, you can be polite but firm in declining a meat dish. Just say, "It looks good, but I don't eat meat." If you're not all right with this approach, then by all means say something. As soon as you are asked to dinner, you can thank the host and say, "Sounds great. Is it all right [or "don't forget"] that I'm a vegetarian?"

What about when you're the host? Should you offer meat to those you know eat it all the time, or cook vegetarian dishes only? You'll probably be happier not serving meat in your own house, especially if you're an ethical vegetarian. Few people would object to not having meat at just one meal. And remember that it's a good way to "show off" vegetarian cuisine. You could bring out some of the standards of veggie fare: savory bean soups, veggie lasagna, bean burritos, or avocado tacos. (You're probably better off saving the tofu and more exotic dishes for your veggie friends.)

You can host a vegetarian meal and show the guests that this food is really good! If you feel like it, pull out all the stops and make a fantastic meal. Why not make food an adventure! After all, many meat eaters have been "converted" to vegetarianism by friends who cook vegetarian meals.

At Restaurants More and more restaurants, especially in urban areas, have begun offering meatless entrées. At many other restaurants, you can fashion a meal out of appetizers, soups, salads, and breads—and fewer people these days think that's odd. If you can't find a vegetarian restaurant, your best bets are ethnic places—Indian, Chinese, Italian, Mexican, and others. If you have doubts about, say, whether the soup stock is chicken or vegetable, just ask. Most waiters are happy to answer questions about the food.

If you don't see something on the menu that you can eat, tell the waiter, "I'm a vegetarian. Is there something the cook could make for me without meat?" In most cases, restaurants are happy to accommodate you, and sometimes will turn out something your dining companions will envy. If you're planning a trip and wondering where you'll eat, try using the computer. Look at the vegetarian

section on the World Wide Web for a list of vegetarian restaurants broken down by region. You can also check out a book called *Vegetarian Journal's Guide to Natural Foods Restaurants in the U.S. and Canada*. Also, look in the Yellow Pages under "Natural Foods," and ask the folks that run the place.

At Fast-Food Places   Times are changing. Used to be that a vegetarian couldn't find anything to eat at a fast-food restaurant. Today, Wendy's has baked potatoes and a large salad bar with plenty of hot and cold options; Taco Bell does not use animal fat in its refried beans; Subway shops offer a cheese and veggie sub (some even offer a vegan burger sub). Other chains such as Burger King are testing meatless burgers. But don't make a habit of fast food, even if it is vegetarian—most of it tends to be high in sodium and low in nutrients, especially when compared with whole foods.

In the Air   Most airlines will give you a veggie meal if you request one at least forty-eight hours in advance, but it's easy for your request to be overlooked unless you're vigilant about tracking it. Here's how to make sure you don't go hungry in the skies. If you have a travel agent, make sure he or she knows that you want vegetarian meals on all flights. (If you eat dairy, make sure to specify this; some airlines are really at a loss trying to feed vegans, and you may get nothing more than a sad-looking salad when they might have given you a cheese omelet or cheese tortellini. Also, many airlines tend to lump vegetarian food with low-fat or "health" food, so you may end up

97

with rice cakes instead of a roll, even though the roll has no animal products in it.)

Get written confirmation from your agent that a vegetarian meal has been ordered. A couple of days before the flight, call the airline to confirm your special meal. When you check in at the airport, mention it to the agent at the counter. Once on the plane, tell the attendant that you have ordered a special meal. Finally, pack a bagel, fruit, or granola just in case.

At Parties   Parties are easier to handle than dinners. After all, the main point of a party is socializing, not eating. When you get an invitation, you might want to ask if you can bring something, and make a point of bringing a healthy snack, like hummus and pita bread with carrot sticks and tomatoes (it's another great opportunity to introduce others to vegetarianism). Classic etiquette says that you should not inform your host about your dietary preferences unless you're asked. Imagine the plight of the host who has to figure out what to serve to a bunch of individuals, each of whom has their own particular food tastes (one doesn't eat mushrooms, another is allergic to wheat, another hates vegetables). You might want to eat something before you go if you're not sure what will be served.

WHAT IF I "SLIP UP?"

You're at grandma's and you eat some vegetable soup cooked with a chicken broth. You scrape the chicken off the chicken-and-biscuits but eat the gravy. You eat a piece of pepperoni pizza. Are you a failure? Not a vegetarian? Kicked out of the club? No! Remember that you control what you eat. There's no pressure, nothing to feel guilty about. Just go on to the next day. And be proud of yourself for paying attention to what goes into your body.

A CRASH COURSE
IN NUTRITION

ten

A BALANCED VEGETARIAN DIET IS FAR HEALTHIER than a diet based on meats and dairy products. But the key word is "balanced." If you replace the meat in your diet only with eggs and cheese, without adding whole grains, beans, vegetables, and fruits, you won't be that much healthier than the typical meat-and-potatoes person. You'll be worse off if you rely on junk food: chips, fried foods, cookies, cake, and a thousand other pitfalls.

Many new vegetarians, young and old, may rely on cheese sandwiches, omelets, cheese pizza, french fries, and perhaps frozen veggie burgers when they're first experimenting with a vegetarian diet. Clearly such foods are not the best (but then neither are burgers, sausage pizza, and fries).

If your parents express concern about your vegetarianism, they are probably worried about your health. They may also have trouble understanding your concerns about animal rights or the environment, but when it comes to your health, they may feel a need to put their foot down. The best way to combat their fears is to know how a healthy vegetarian diet works, so that you can explain it to them.

This chapter reviews the ideas behind nutrition guidelines, the basics of good nutrition, and the common pitfalls of vegetarian diets and easy ways to avoid them. The most important thing to remember: a good vegetarian diet is perfectly healthy for young people.

We'll start with a discussion of the stuff your body needs—vitamins, minerals, and other nutrients—and we'll give particular attention to those things of concern to vegetarians.

PROTEIN

When it comes to protein, there are so many misconceptions it's hard to know where to start. Some of the myths:

- Meat is the only source of protein.
- Meat is the best source of protein.
- Protein makes you strong.
- Vegetarians have to combine foods to get complete protein.
- The more protein, the better.
- Vegetarians have a hard time getting enough protein.

Let's debunk these myths one by one. First off, meat is not the only source of protein. In fact, all foods contain protein except fruit, sugars, and alcohol (even fruit has a little). Protein is found in bread, pasta, rice, vegetables, beans, tofu, and other foods.

A good, or "superior," source of protein is one that is easily absorbed by the body and provides essential amino acids. Although plant proteins are not digested as easily as animal proteins, they are digested easily enough to make them a good source. And though it is true that animal protein is a "complete" protein—that is, it supplies all the amino acids—eating a variety of plant proteins will give us "complete" protein, too. You will have no problem getting all the right proteins unless you limit your diet to, say, nothing but potatoes (and why would you want to do that?).

Protein is important, but it does not build muscle or provide energy. It is exercise that makes you strong. Energy is provided by carbohydrates such as bread, pasta, and rice. (This is what athletes are doing when they say they're "carbo-loading.") So what does protein do? It helps you see and think, makes up and repairs bone and muscle tissue, regulates your hormones and enzymes, and helps fight infections.

The theory that vegetarians have to combine foods to create a "complete" protein was started by Frances Moore Lappé's book *Diet for a Small Planet*, which has influenced many people to become vegetarian. In the early editions of her book, Lappé spoke of the need to combine food such as rice and beans in a meal. The idea is that protein is made up of nine essential amino acids, and that some foods provide only some of these amino acids. But scientists now know that if these foods are eaten at any time over the course of a few days, your body will combine them to make complete protein. In any case, complementary proteins have a tendency to go together in many dishes: beans and rice or corn chips, or pasta and cheese (soy or dairy) or a vegetable sauce. The most "complete" protein comes from combining legumes such as black-eyed peas, chickpeas, peanuts, lentils, sprouts, and beans (black, kidney, lima, navy) with grains such as rice, wheat, corn, rye, bulgur, oats, millet, barley, and buckwheat.

More is not better in the case of protein. Research shows too much protein can be a contributing factor in many major diseases, especially protein that comes from animal sources (meat, milk, and dairy products). Animal protein and plant protein differ in the concentration of protein (it's more concentrated in the animal protein) and the amino acids they contain. Excess protein has been linked to an increased risk of coronary disease, cancer, and diabetes. (See chapter seven for details of these risks). Growing teenagers need 44–59 grams of protein a day. Most Americans get 90–120 grams a day—far more than is needed.

Protein deficiency is virtually unheard of in this country, even among vegetarians. The only way to be deficient in protein would be not to eat enough calories for your energy needs. The message once again: eat a variety of good, whole foods and you'll fill this need.

CALCIUM

Quick, name a nondairy calcium source! Most people equate calcium with milk, but in fact there are plenty of other ways to get it. There's nothing wrong with drinking milk in moderation, if that's part of your diet, but an unlimited quantity is unhealthy, especially whole and 2 percent milk. Why? It's full of fat.

So what are the alternatives to milk? Calcium is not as concentrated in other foods as in milk. But calcium-set tofu, leafy green vegetables, and Chinese cabbage are good sources. You need about 1.2 servings of tofu (the type processed with calcium sulfate) to equal the amount of calcium in a serving of milk. You need 2.3 times the servings of Chinese cabbage; 2.6 times the amount of mustard greens; and 1.9 times the amount of turnip greens. Also, look for calcium-fortified fruit juices (they're pretty common now) and calcium-fortified soy, almond, or rice milks, seeds (such as sesame), broccoli, legumes (dried peas and beans such as split peas), figs, blackstrap molasses, and tortillas processed with lime.

For teenagers, the recommended daily allowance of calcium is 1,200 milligrams. To get that much without consuming dairy products, you would need to eat all of the following: one cup each of cooked mustard greens, broccoli, and Chinese cabbage; one corn tortilla; a small piece of calcium sulfate-processed tofu; two tablespoons of whole brown sesame seeds; and a glass of calcium-fortified orange juice.

Caffeine and phosphates keep your body from absorbing calcium properly. So keep the soft drinks to a minimum, or try some of the caffeine-free, naturally sweetened sodas found at health food stores.

ZINC

This trace mineral helps build and repair tissue. In general, vegetarians get less zinc than do omnivores, and non-meat sources of zinc are less available to the body. The Loma Linda study of vegetarian teens showed that young vegetarians got about half the recommended daily allowance. (You should know, however, that teenage omnivores also get less zinc than they should.) A zinc deficiency is marked by slow wound healing, nervous disorders, and an impaired sense of taste and smell. Zinc is found in beans, nuts, and seeds such as garbanzo beans (chickpeas), black-eyed peas, lentils, lima beans, green peas, fortified breakfast cereals, oatmeal, brown rice, wheat germ, pumpkin and sunflower seeds, and low-fat milk.

IRON

Iron intake is another concern for many vegetarians, because meat is the most concentrated source. But studies have shown that vegetarians are no more likely to get anemia than meat eaters (although female teenage vegetarians are more likely to have reduced iron stores due to iron lost during menstruation). Milk is a poor source of iron, and eggs have iron that the body cannot use well, so vegans are not at an increased risk for deficiency. But all of us should be sure we're getting the right amount. Iron deficiency is a common nutritional problem around the world, especially in developing nations. In the United States, anemia has not been as much of a problem since the introduction of iron-enriched foods (cereals, breads, pastas) and iron supplements. Iron deficiency can cause fatigue, less than peak athletic performance, impaired thinking and reasoning skills, and an inability to retain body heat.

Good sources of iron are whole-grain and fortified cereals (check labels), legumes, dark green vegetables, nuts, seeds, and dried fruits (figs, dates, raisins, and prunes). Just a single serving of Rice Chex, for example, will provide you with 50 percent of your iron needs for a day. Also, cooking in an old-fashioned iron pot greatly increases the amount of iron in food. You can increase the amount of iron in spaghetti sauce (a low-iron food) *twenty-nine times* by cooking it in an iron pot for three hours. Even fried potatoes cooked for thirty minutes gain eight times the iron when they are cooked in an iron pan. Vitamin C also helps boost the amount of iron you get—just add a glass of orange juice, a few slices of tomato, or leafy greens to your meal to get the effect.

Before deciding to take an iron supplement, check with a doctor or nutritionist—too much iron can be harmful. Some scientists have associated it with increased rates of heart attack and colon cancer. In general, it is better to get your vitamins and minerals from food, not from supplements.

CARBOHYDRATES

Athletes like to "carbo-load" before a big event—essentially they eat a ton of grains or rices. That's because carbohydrates—found in starchy foods such as breads, cereals, pasta, beans, potatoes, corn, or winter squash—provide fuel for our bodies. In the old days people thought carbohydrates were fattening, but we now know that they are easily burned up by the body. Complex carbohydrates—basically unrefined foods—work best. White rice, white flour, and white sugar, and foods made of them, are not used by the body as efficiently as whole grains and brown rice. Stick to unrefined, whole foods as much as possible.

FAT

What's fat doing in a discussion of good stuff our body needs? Well, we actually need *some* fat to keep out bodies working right. We wouldn't want to cut it out altogether. Fats (in the form of milk, cheese, eggs, butter, oils, nuts, peanut butter, avocados, etc.) help make us feel full longer because they slow the emptying of the stomach, and they transport vitamins A, D, E, and K. We also need the fatty acid called linoleic acid. This is an essential nutrient for the nervous system.

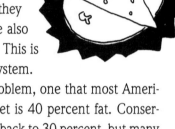

But too much fat is definitely a problem, one that most Americans have. The average American's diet is 40 percent fat. Conservative nutritionists recommend cutting back to 30 percent, but many others are convinced that our diets should be no more than 10 percent fat if we want to be healthy and most resistant to disease.

There are two kinds of fats: saturated (found mainly in animal products and in coconut and palm oil) and unsaturated (oils such as safflower, sunflower, soybean, corn, oil, peanut, and canola). Saturated fats often mean higher levels of cholesterol in the blood, and high blood cholesterol is one of the clear risk factors for heart disease. You are avoiding much fat by cutting meat, fish, and poultry from your diet, but if you replace those foods with things like cheese, fried foods, eggs, and yogurt, you could still be getting too much.

FIBER

Fiber is not just an old person's concern. Also called "roughage," this is the stuff that keeps your digestive system running smoothly. A vegetarian diet—with plenty of whole wheat, oats, beans, vegetables, and fruits—provides plenty of fiber. The FDA (Food and Drug Administration) continues to study the possibility of a link between a high-fiber diet and lower rates of some types of cancer. The kind of fiber found in oats, carrots, fruits, and beans is thought to lower blood cholesterol.

VITAMINS D AND B$_{12}$

Of all vitamins necessary for good human health, only two are not provided by plant foods, vitamins D and B$_{12}$. Getting enough vitamin D, which helps our bodies absorb calcium, is an easy proposition. A few minutes' exposure to the sun provides us with all the vitamin D we need. Our bodies are able to store excess vitamin D for some time, so we can usually get all we need during the summer months to last us through the winter. Because we need so little, there is no recommended daily allowance for it. Vitamin D is also found in eggs, butter, buttermilk, and fortified milk. Too much vitamin D can cause dangerous levels of calcium to store up in the body, causing kidney problems. So do not use a vitamin supplement unless you are a vegan who rarely gets out into the sun, or unless your doctor prescribes it.

Perhaps no vitamin gets as much attention in vegetarian literature as B$_{12}$: this essential vitamin is only found in animal foods. It is found in milk, cheese, eggs, and other dairy products, so only vegans (total vegetarians) need to worry about supplementing their diet to get B$_{12}$. Some nutritionists believe that sea vegetables, mushrooms, and tempeh (a fermented soy product) contain B$_{12}$, but most others believe there is no reliable source of the vitamin outside of animal products. That's because our bodies can't use most of the B$_{12}$ found in these plant foods.

Even if you rarely eat dairy products or drink milk you'll be getting enough B$_{12}$, because we need very little of it. Our daily requirement is just two-millionths of a gram a day. (One glass of milk and one egg provide this amount.) The body has the ability to absorb and store B$_{12}$ for two to three years, so new vegans needn't worry much about not getting enough.

106

Most cases of B_{12} deficiency occur among people who, for one reason or another, cannot absorb the vitamin. It's not that they're not getting enough of the vitamin from their food, but that their bodies don't take it in. The elderly are more prone to this problem.

It is important not to downplay the importance of B_{12}. A deficiency can result in damage to your central nervous system and even death. If you're a vegan, look for B_{12} in many ready-to-eat cereals (Rice Chex and NutriGrain, among others). Some breads, pastas, and crackers are fortified with B_{12}—check labels. Unfortunately, B_{12} isn't always listed on the label, even when it is present; if you like a particular cereal or bread a lot, write to the company to find out.

Some nutritional yeast flakes are also a source of B_{12}. Look for the Red Star T6635 brand. (Nutritional yeast flakes taste a bit like grated Parmesan cheese and can be added to soups and stews, or sprinkled on popcorn.) Some soy foods such as soy burgers, soy dogs, or "fake bacon" also contain B_{12}. If you don't find a favorite source of it in these foods, you can take a supplement. Contrary to what some vegans think, B_{12} supplements do not come from liver; they are taken from bacterial cultures. Note that it may be best to take a B_{12} supplement separately rather than as part of a multivitamin. The body seems to absorb it better when it's by itself.

Here is a handy list of vegetarian sources of nutrients commonly found in animal foods:

Vitamin B_{12}: fortified soy milk and cereals, nutritional yeast
Vitamin D: fortified foods and sunshine
Calcium: tofu, broccoli, seeds, nuts, kale, bok choy, legumes (dried peas and beans such as split peas), greens, calcium-enriched grain products, and tortillas processed with lime
Iron: legumes, tofu, green leafy vegetables (spinach, kale, mustard greens, collard greens), dried fruit, whole grains, and iron-fortified cereals and breads, especially whole wheat; iron absorption is improved by vitamin C, found in citrus fruits and juices (orange, lemon, lime, grapefruit), tomatoes, strawberries, broccoli, peppers, dark green leafy vegetables, and potatoes with skins

Daily Food Guide for Vegetarians

(reprinted by permission from the American Dietetic Association)

FOOD GROUP	DAILY SERVINGS	SERVING SIZES
Breads, cereals, rice, pasta	6 or more	1 slice of bread 1/2 bun, bagel, or English muffin 1/2 cup cooked cereal, rice, or pasta 1 ounce dry cereal
Vegetables	4 or more	1/2 cup cooked or 1 cup raw
Legumes and other meat substitutes	2 to 3	1/2 cup cooked beans 4 ounces tofu or tempeh 8 ounces soy milk 2 tablespoons nuts or seeds (they're high in fat so use sparingly)
Fruits	3 or more	1 piece fresh 3/4 cup juice 1/2 cup canned or cooked
Dairy products	optional— up to 3	1 cup low-fat or skim milk 1 cup low-fat or non-fat yogurt 1 1/2 ounce low-fat cheese

FOOD GROUP	DAILY SERVINGS	SERVING SIZES
Eggs	optional—limit to 3–4 yolks per week	1 egg or 2 egg whites
Fats, sweets	go easy on these foods	oil, margarine, and mayonnaise cakes, cookies, pies, pastries, and candies

The Physicians Committee for Responsible Medicine, a group of prominent U.S. physicians, has proposed this new basic food group chart for vegetarians:

Whole Grains	5 or more servings daily
Vegetables	3 or more servings daily
Fruits	3 or more servings daily
Legumes	2 or 3 servings daily

U.S. Government's Recommended Daily Allowances for Adolescents (Ages 11–18)

Energy	2200 calories (females)
	2500 calories (males, ages 11–14)
	3000 calories (males, ages 15–18)
Protein	45–46 grams (ages 11–14)
	44 grams (females, ages 15–18)
	59 grams (males, ages 15–18)
Calcium	1200 milligrams
Iron	15 milligrams
Zinc	15 milligrams
Vitamin B_{12}	2 micrograms

Going Veg.
The American Dietetic Association
Recommends:

1. minimizing intake of less nutritious foods such as sweets and fatty foods

2. choosing whole or unrefined grain products instead of refined products (for example: whole wheat bread and pasta instead of white bread and pasta; brown rice instead of white rice)

3. choosing a variety of nuts, seeds, legumes, fruits, and vegetables, including good sources of vitamin C to improve iron absorption

4. choosing low-fat varieties of milk products

5. avoiding excessive cholesterol intake by limiting eggs to two or three yolks a week

6. for vegans, using properly fortified food sources of vitamin B_{12}, such as fortified soy milks or cereals, or taking a supplement

7. for infants, children, and teenagers, ensuring adequate intake of calories, iron, and vitamin D, taking supplements if needed

8. consulting a registered dietitian or other nutrition professional, especially during periods of growth or recovery from illness

To find a nutrition professional who is well versed in current vegetarian diets, contact your state or local dietetic association, or call the American and Dietetic Association at 1-800-366-1655. Many other organizations can provide information about vegetarian diets. See the list of resources at the back of this book.

Total vegetarians (vegans) need to be sure to eat some foods that are dense in calories to meet their energy needs. Some such foods are dried peas and beans, nuts and nut butters, dried fruits, whole grains, and seeds.

The following list demonstrates how easy it is to get the important nutrients some people think are lacking in a vegetarian diet. Note that some foods, such as blackstrap molasses, are an excellent source of both calcium and iron. Note, too, that we haven't included protein sources, since, as discussed above, it's easy to get all the protein you need from just about any combination of foods.

Calcium Sources

Collard greens, one cup cooked	357 mg
Calcium-fortified orange juice, 8 ounces	300 mg
Blackstrap molasses, two tablespoons	274 mg
Firm tofu processed with calcium sulfate, 4 ounces	250–350 mg
Turnip greens, one cup cooked	250 mg
Kale, one cup cooked	180 mg
Broccoli, one cup cooked	178 mg
Sesame seeds, two tablespoons	176 mg
Calcium-fortified soy milk, 8 ounces	160–300 mg
Chinese cabbage, one cup cooked	158 mg

Iron Sources

Millet, 1/2 cup cooked	7.0 mg
Blackstrap molasses, 2 tablespoons	6.4 mg
Kidney beans, 1/2 cup cooked	3.33 mg
Pinto beans, 1/2 cup cooked	2.85 mg
Chickpeas, 1/2 cup cooked	2.55 mg
Seitan, 4 ounces	4.0 mg
Swiss chard, 1 cup cooked	4.0 mg
Lentils, 1/2 cup cooked	3.3 mg
Spinach, 1 cup cooked	3.2 mg

Potato, baked, with skin	2.8 mg
Sesame seeds, 2 tablespoons	2.6 mg
Figs, 5 medium	2.1 mg
Tofu: 3 1/2 ounces	1.0–9.6 mg
(varies among types—check labels)	
Black beans, 1/2 cup cooked	1.7 mg

(And don't forget that a good way to boost your iron intake is to eat plenty of vitamin C–rich foods, such as orange, cranberry, or grapefruit juice, red and green peppers, cantaloupe, kale, broccoli, tomatoes, and potatoes.)

Zinc Sources

Chickpeas (garbanzo beans), 1/2 cup cooked	1.31 mg
Sesame seeds, 2 tablespoons	1.65 mg
Black-eyed peas, 1/2 cup cooked	1.61 mg
Lentils, 1/2 cup cooked	.94 mg
Sunflower seeds, 2 tablespoons	.867 mg
Wheat germ, 1 tablespoon	.687 mg
Fortified breakfast cereals	see labels

Source: The New Laurel's Kitchen

HOW DO VEGETARIAN TEENS FARE?

Though vegetarianism is growing fast among teenagers, there are few studies that have examined the effects of vegetarian diets on adolescents and their growth. Most studies about young vegetarians have focused on preschool children. And many studies focus solely on restrictive diets such as veganism and macrobiotics. In the late 1970s, however, researchers studied eight thousand children ages eight through eighteen attending Seventh-Day Adventist and public schools in California. Seventh-Day Adventists are largely vegetarian, do not smoke or drink alcohol, and tend to stay away from soda pop and other beverages containing caffeine. About one-third of the Seventh-Day Adventist students were classified as lacto-ovo vegetarians (they said they ate meat less than once per week; they did consume eggs and dairy products). The results of the Loma Linda Child-Adolescent Study, reported in the medical journal *Adolescent Medicine*, were quite promising for young people wanting to follow a vegetarian diet and remain healthy.

You might expect that kids who don't eat meat would wind up eating other fatty, high-cholesterol foods such as eggs and cheese. In the Loma Linda study, though, the omnivores (meat eaters) ate more dairy products and eggs than the vegetarians. The vegetarians did not replace meat with meat analogues (veggie burgers, tofu dogs) either. Instead, they ate many more fruits, vegetables, and starchy foods such as breads, cereals, pasta, and rice.

The report found that vegetarian teens consumed less saturated fat than their meat-eating counterparts. Not surprisingly, they were also leaner. The vegetarians had no trouble meeting the recommended daily allowance of protein and vitamin B_{12}.

The vegetarians in the study had less than optimal intake of other important minerals. Vegetarian females aged fifteen to eighteen received only 72 percent of the recommended daily allowance of calcium. All the other groups got more calcium than they needed. Iron was found to be lacking, but this was also a problem with omnivores. Female vegetarians took in 80 percent of the recommended daily allowance, while female meat eaters got 86 percent—not a significant difference. Getting enough zinc was also a problem among vegetarians, especially females aged fifteen to eighteen. Zinc intake among omnivores ranged from 83 percent to 107 percent of the recommended daily allowance; among vegetarians the intake was 40 percent to 69 percent of the recommendations.

Zinc is important for growth, so we would assume that since vegetarians get less zinc than omnivores, they would be shorter. Not so. A study of these children, in fact, showed that the Seventh-Day Adventist vegetarian children were taller than their meat-eating classmates. Other studies have shown that children raised on vegan or macrobiotic diets grow more slowly than omnivores until about age five, but that they catch up by age ten.

A special note: Some adolescents, especially girls, have used vegetarianism to cover up an eating disorder, such as anorexia nervosa. These girls eat very little and are overly concerned with being thin. They may say they are vegetarian so that no one will discover the reason they're picking at their food. Of course, not everyone who becomes a vegetarian should be suspected of anorexia. It is something to be aware of, however, especially if someone is obsessed with the food they eat and their weight.

eleven

REAL FOOD FOR REAL VEGETARIANS

IT'S EASY TO EAT A HEALTHFUL VEGETARIAN DIET IF you've got the right foods on hand. Here are some good foods to keep stocked in the pantry:

- ready-to-eat, whole-grain breakfast cereals
- quick-cooking whole-grain cereals, such as oatmeal
- whole-grain breads (can be frozen—simply pop slices into the toaster to thaw), bagels, and crackers, such as rye, whole wheat, or multigrain
- other grains, such as barley and bulgur wheat
- canned beans, such as pintos, black beans, kidney beans, or garbanzos (also called chickpeas)
- rice (brown, wild, white)
- pastas
- corn or flour tortillas (these freeze well)
- vegetarian soups (lentil, minestrone)

- ramen noodle soups (look for the kind that's baked, not fried, and made with brown rice; add cooked vegetables for an easy meal)
- plain frozen vegetables
- tomato sauce
- frozen fruit juice concentrates
- nut spreads, such as peanut or almond butter or tahini (sesame seed spread)
- canned or frozen fruit (packed in its own juice with no added sugar)

All that is good for you, and some of it may be obvious, but you need some spice in your life, too! Following are some vegetarian foods you may not be as familiar with:

Tofu

This much-maligned staple of the vegetarian diet is made from soybeans, or "bean curd" (that's what they call it on Chinese menus).

 It is sold in tubs of water or in aseptic boxes that last a long time without refrigeration. Tofu doesn't really have a taste of its own—it absorbs spices, soy sauce, etc. It's made from soybean milk that's hardened into blocks with a mineral salt. Use the firm or extra firm for cubing and adding to stir-fries and stews, and grilling on the barbecue. Use the soft and silken type, mashed, for salad dressings, "cheese" cake, and other desserts. Look for tofu hot dogs in the freezer case of health-food stores and co-ops.

Tempeh

Tempeh is made from tofu, but it is actually fermented soybeans shaped into a soybean "cake." It has a different texture—more like meat, in fact—and can be cooked like a burger, cubed and thrown into stir-fries, or cooked with a gravy. Tempeh is particularly popular in Indonesia.

Miso

Miso has been called the beef bouillon of vegetarian cooking. This paste, made from soybeans and grains, adds a rich flavor to soups, sauces, and gravies. It comes in dark (strong-tasting) and light (not so strong and sort of sweet) varieties.

Tamari

Like soy sauce, only brewed naturally.

TVP

Textured Vegetable Protein (TVP) can satisfy a hankering for "meat." It is made from soy flour from which the oil has been removed. You buy it dry, in tiny granules, flakes, and chunks. Just add boiling water, and you've got fake meat.

Seitan

Often called "wheat meat," seitan is made from wheat flour kneaded with water, rolled into a large ball, and boiled. It comes in chunks seasoned in broth, or frozen, and can take the place of chicken, beef, or barbecued ribs. You can barbecue it and prepare like any meat. Seitan is also used to make fake lunch meat.

Meat Look-alikes

Veggie burgers, veggie franks, fake sausage, fake chicken—all are made to look and taste (somewhat) like meat. They are made from soy, wheat gluten, vegetables, and nuts. Most are sold frozen, though veggie burgers also come in a dry mix—you add water and an egg (optional).

Nutritional Yeast
This powder tastes a bit like grated Parmesan cheese. Sprinkle on popcorn or add to soups and salads. Some brands are a good source of vitamin B_{12}.

Cow's Milk Substitutes
Soy milk uses soy protein as a base. It may be flavored. Soy milk is an acquired taste; some people think it is too sweet. Look for brands that are fortified with vitamins A, B_{12}, and D, as well as calcium, to get the same nutritional benefits you'd get from cow's milk. Also look for milk-like drinks made of rice and almonds. These are often vitamin-fortified as well.

Tahini
A spread made from sesame seeds (it looks like light-colored peanut butter). This Middle Eastern food is often mixed with lemon juice and garlic to flavor vegetables and legumes.

Hummus
A thick dip or spread made from chickpeas, garlic, lemon juice, and tahini. It is common in the Middle East. It's usually spread on toasted pita bread and eaten with tomatoes, or used as a dip for carrot sticks or other raw vegetables.

Alternatives to Eggs in Baking—replace one egg with:
- one banana (great for cakes and pancakes)
- two tablespoons cornstarch or arrowroot (starch that comes from the arrowroot plant)
- 1/4 cup tofu (blend tofu with liquids in recipe)
- or use a commercial, prepared egg replacer, such as Ener-G Egg Replacer.

One more quick tip:
Add bulk and texture to vegetarian chilis and soups by adding bul-

gur, which is a fine grain made of wheat. It will make your meal more satisfying.

The Savvy Label Reader: How to Spot Hidden Animal Ingredients

Things are not always what they seem. That vegetable soup you're buying may well have a chicken stock. The crackers you're eating may have animal fat in them. Alas, even soy cheese may have an animal product in it.

If you're a vegan and want to avoid all animal products, you've got to become a reader of labels—and know what to look for. Here are some common hidden animal ingredients:

Albumin   Derived from egg whites, this substance is used as a thickener or to add texture to some cereals, ready-made frostings, and puddings.

Anchovies   Look for them as an ingredient in almost all Worcestershire sauces and in Caesar salads.

Animal shortening   Just another name for animal fat, such shortening is found in processed foods such as cookies, crackers, and snack cakes. This is stuff you shouldn't be eating anyway. If you're not into reading labels, get your crackers and other snacks at a health-food store or co-op.

Casein   Sometimes appears as "caseinate" on labels, this milk protein is added to most soy cheeses to improve the texture and to make it melt better. It's used in other "nondairy" products, too.

Gelatin   Made from animal bones. Look for it as an ingredient in marshmallows, nonfat yogurts, and roasted peanuts. "Kosher" gelatin is usually vegetarian. There are some vegan marshmallows, too.

Lard   Animal fat. Used in most refried beans, though there are vegetarian varieties (usually prominently labeled).

Rennet   Often just listed as "enzymes," rennet comes from the lining of calves' stomachs and is used to make cheese. Look for labels on cheese that say "rennets" or "enzymes."

Whey   A milk product found in many processed foods.

Animal products are not just found in food. They're everywhere, and sometimes nearly impossible to avoid. Shampoos often contain collagen, placenta, animal proteins, and keratin—all animal products. In most soaps you'll find tallow from beef fat. Collagen-based adhesives are found in wallpaper, glues, bandages, emery boards, and plaster board. Gelatin is used in ice cream, candies, yogurt, mayonnaise, and other foods, and also in photographic film. Beef fat and fatty acids are used in shoe cream, crayons, floor wax, cosmetics, deodorants, and detergents.

If you're tempted to throw up your hands in despair of avoiding all animal products, don't worry. There are things you can do to make it easier:

- Shop at natural foods stores or a co-op, which are more likely to carry animal-free products (both food and nonfood).
- Eat whole foods. Avoid processed foods, canned soups, snacks, mixes, and the like.
- Contact People for the Ethical Treatment of Animals (PETA) for a list of products with and without animal products. PETA, P.O. Box 42516, Washington, D.C. 20015.

Can't find vegetarian foods in your local grocery store? Miles away from a co-op or natural foods store? You can shop by catalog. Try one of these:

Garden Spot Distributors, 438 White Oak Road, New Holland, Pennsylvania 17557; (800) 829-5100

Heartland Foods, R.R. 2, Box 189B, Susquehanna, Pennsylvania 18847; (717) 879-8790

Jaffe Bros., P.O. Box 636, Valley Center, California 92082-0636; (619) 749-1133

Mail Order Catalog, P.O. Box 180, Summertown, Tennessee 38483; (800) 695-2241

Shiloh Farms, 1 Hilber Street, Sulphur Springs, Arkansas 72768; (501) 298-3297

Walnut Acres, Penns Creek, Pennsylvania 17862; (717) 837-0601

COOKBOOKS

As recently as twenty-five years ago, it would have been hard to find a vegetarian cookbook. Today, the shelves at your local bookstore are filled with them. Without a doubt, the best overall vegetarian cookbook for beginners (and for more experienced cooks, for that matter) is *The New Laurel's Kitchen* by Laurel Robertson, Carol Flinders, and Brian Ruppenthal (Ten Speed Press, 1986). *Laurel's Kitchen* was initially published in 1976, one of the first vegetarian cookbooks published in America. This updated version goes easier on the cheese and milk in its recipes. But the easy-to-follow recipes aren't the only appeal to this book. It also gives tips on cooking techniques; buying and storing fruits, vegetables, and grains; a comprehensive section on vegetarian nutrition; and menu suggestions.

Another excellent choice in the same category is the *Moosewood Cookbook* by Mollie Katzen (Ten Speed Press, 1992). This cookbook has also been revised since its first publication in 1977, and recipes are now lighter.

For vegans, two books stand out: *The New Farm Vegetarian Cookbook* by Louise Hagler and Dorothy R. Bates (Book Publishing Company, 1988) provides a lot of basic information about soyfoods and vegan nutrition, along with plenty of hearty recipes low in salt, fat, and sugar. *Simply Vegan* by Debra Wasserman and Reed Mangels (Vegetarian Resource Group, 1991) lives up to its title's promise: simple recipes ideal for a beginning cook.

If you're looking for a good ethnic vegetarian book, and you've got some basic cooking knowledge, check out *Lord Krishna's Cuisine: The Art of Indian Vegetarian Cooking* by Yamuna Devi (Bala Books, 1987). It is the first vegetarian cookbook ever to win an award from the International Association of Cooking Professionals.

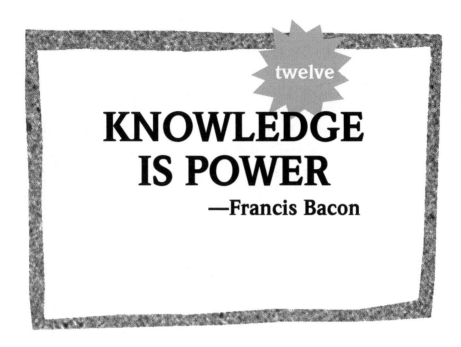

twelve

KNOWLEDGE IS POWER

—Francis Bacon

CONVINCED THAT VEGETARIANISM IS THE RIGHT thing to do? Want to learn more, spread the message, or work for change? Here's what you can do:

CELEBRATE

March 20: Great American Meatout Day
Mother's Day: National Veal Ban Action Day
October 1: World Vegetarian Day
October 2: World Farm Animals Day
Contact the Farm Animal Reform Movement (301-530-1237) or the North American Vegetarian Society (518-568-7970) for more information on how you can participate.

SHARE IT ON THE SMALL SCREEN

Videos are for rent from the North American Vegetarian Society, P.O. Box 72, Dolgeville, New York 13329 (518-568-7970). Rental is free, with a deposit and $3 for postage and handling costs.

"Food Without Fear." 20-minute overview of vegetarian issues. Looks at factory farming, health, the environment, and poverty in developing nations.

"The Vegetarian World." 29 minutes. Narrated by William Shatner. Features famous vegetarians talking about health, economics, and social conscience reasons to quit eating meat.

"Healthy, Wealthy, and Wise." 30 minutes.

"Voices I Have Heard." 55 minutes. Documentary about the contributions of older Americans to the animal rights movement.

"We Are All Noah." 30 minutes. Explores the relationship of religion to animal rights. Specifically examines the ethical teachings of Christianity and Judaism.

"The Animals Film." The first documentary to thoroughly explore the forms of animal exploitation, from factory farming to vivisection. Narrated by Julie Christie. Graphic presentation may be disturbing.

"In Defense of Animals." 28 minutes. A portrait of philosopher Peter Singer and his theories about animal rights. Includes a brief history of the animal rights movement.

"The Making of Turkey." 17 minutes. Exposes the cruelty and unhealthy conditions endured by domestic turkeys.

GO ON-LINE

There's a wealth of veggie information on the Internet and the World Wide Web. All you need is a computer, modem, and on-line service such as America Online, CompuServe, Delphi, Geni, or Prodigy. You'll find a variety of features, such as cooking and recipe information, health, environment, and animal-rights news, and chat groups of all kinds. Say you're looking for a vegetarian restaurant in Cincinnati, where you'll be spending the summer. You could go on-line and ask fellow veggies for advice. It's a great way to get information and to get in touch with other vegetarians. Two Usenet newsgroups to check out: **rec.food.veg** and **rec.food.veg.cooking**.

JOIN

There are two types of vegetarian organizations. Local groups represent a city or state and exist also to provide support and a social outlet for members. Events can include potluck dinners, picnics, lectures, and cooking demonstrations. To find a local group near you, call the Vegetarian Awareness Network at 800-234-8343. Once you find a local group, ask about starting or joining a youth group within the organization.

National groups provide education and work toward changing attitudes and policies nationwide. Some focus on all types of vegetarian issues; others target specific subjects such as animal rights.

Vegetarian Youth Network is a support network open to vegetarian teens (between the ages of twelve and nineteen). For more information, send a self-addressed stamped envelope to Tovah Walters-Gidseg, c/o the Vegetarian Youth Network, 62 Plains Road, New Paltz, New York 12561, or e-mail her:
tjre18b@prodigy.com.

North American Vegetarian Society
P.O. Box 72
Dolgeville, New York 13329
(518) 568-7970
Publishes an excellent free booklet called "The Care and Feeding of a Vegetarian." Get one for your parents!

American Vegan Society
P.O. Box H

Malaga, New Jersey 08328-0908
(609) 694-2887

Vegan Action
P.O. Box 4353
Berkeley, California 94704-0353
(510) 843-6343
email: **vegan@mellers1.pysch.berkeley.edu**

Vegetarian Resource Group
P.O. Box 1463
Baltimore, Maryland 21203
(410) 366-VEGE [8343]
This nonprofit educational organization provides several useful pamphlets for free. Send a self-addressed, stamped envelope for each pamphlet desired: Vegetarian Nutrition, Vegetarianism in a Nutshell, Veganism in a Nutshell, Vegetarianism and the Environment, What Is Animal Rights?, and Hints for Starting a Vegetarian/Environmental/Animal Rights Group at Your School or College (send a self-addressed envelope with two first-class stamps for this one).

A student membership, which includes a subscription to the bimonthly *Vegetarian Journal*, costs $14.

This group also awards a $50 savings bond to the winner of its annual essay contest. Entries must be postmarked by May 1. Contact the group for details. Also contact the group for a complete list of books, pamphlets, posters, bumper stickers, T-shirts, and postcards.

Vegetarian Union of North America
P.O. Box 9710
Washington, D.C. 20016

Vegetarian Education Network (VE-Net)
P.O. Box 3347

West Chester, Pennsylvania 19381
(717) 529-8638
This group publishes *How On Earth!,* a magazine for teen vegetarians. It also promotes the teaching of vegetarian issues in schools.

Health Groups

The American Dietetic Association
216 West Jackson Boulevard
Chicago, Illinois 60606-6995
(312) 899-0040
Write for a copy of the pamphlet "Eating Well—The Vegetarian Way."

Physicians Committee for Responsible Medicine
5100 Wisconsin Avenue, Suite 404
Washington, D.C. 20016
(202) 686-2210
Among other activities, this group lobbies the United States Department of Agriculture to change its dietary guidelines to reflect current scientific literature that supports a plant-based diet.

Center for Science in the Public Interest
1875 Connecticut Avenue, N.W., Suite 300
Washington, D.C. 20009-5728
(202) 265-4954

Animal Rights Groups

American Anti-Vivisection Society
801 Old York Road, Suite 204
Jenkintown, Pennsylvania 19046-1685
(215) 887-0816
Sponsors Animalearn, a series of summer programs on animals rights aimed at students.

Beauty Without Cruelty
175 West 12th Street, 12G
New York, New York 10011
(212) 989-8073
They provide a list of cosmetics firms that do not test their products on animals.

Compassion in World Farming
20 Lavant Street
Petersfield, Hants
England

Farm Animal Reform Movement
P.O. Box 30654
Bethesda, Maryland 20824
(301) 530-1737

Farm Sanctuary
P.O. Box 150
Watkins Glen, New York 14891-0150
(607) 583-2225

The Fund for Animals
850 Sligo Avenue, Suite LL2
Silver Spring, Maryland 20901
(301) 585-2591

Humane Farming Association
1550 California Street, Suite 6
San Francisco, California 94109
(415) 485-1495

Humane Society of the United States
2100 L Street, N.W.

Washington, D.C. 20037
(202) 452-1100

People for the Ethical Treatment of Animals (PETA)
P.O. Box 42516
Washington, D.C. 20015
(301) 770-7444

Progressive Animal Welfare Society
P.O. Box 1037
Lynnwood, Washington 98046
(206) 743-3845

United Poultry Concerns
P.O. Box 59367
Potomac, Maryland 20859
(301) 948-2406

World Hunger Groups

American Friends Service Committee
1501 Cherry Street
Philadelphia, Pennsylvania 19102
(215) 241-7000

Food First
145 Ninth Street
San Francisco, California 94103
(415) 864-8555

Institute for Agriculture and Trade Policy
1313 Fifth Street, S.E. #303
Minneapolis, Minnesota 55104
(612) 379-5980

Oxfam America
115 Broadway
Boston, Massachusetts 02116
(617) 482-1211

Environmental Organizations

EarthSave
P.O. Box 68
Santa Cruz, California 95063-0068
(408) 423-4069
Founded by John Robbins, author of *May All Be Fed* and *Diet for a New America*. Primarily an environmental group, but one that also promotes vegetarianism. Offers books, video and audio tapes, speaking tours, seminars, workshops, wilderness outings, local support and action groups, and school nutrition and environmental programs. Sponsors the Healthy School Lunch Program, which gives tips on how to get vegetarian food into your school cafeteria.

Earth Island Institute
300 Broadway, Suite 28
San Francisco, California 94133-3312
(415) 788-3666

Friends of the Earth
530 Seventh Street, S.E.
Washington, D.C. 20003
(202) 543-4312

Vegetarianism and World Religions

Interfaith Council for the Protection of Animals and Nature
4290 Raintree Lane NW
Atlanta, Georgia 30327
(404) 252-9176

International Network for Religion and Animals
P.O. Box 1335
North Wales, Pennsylvania 19454-0335
(215) 721-1908

SUBSCRIBE

Vegetarian magazines keep you up to date on current issues, trends, and nutrition news.

Ahimsa, 501 Old Harding Highway, Malaga, New Jersey 08328. The American Vegan Society publishes this quarterly magazine on ethical issues.

How on Earth! P.O. Box 3347, West Chester, Pennsylvania 19381. Written by teens, for teens. Covers all aspects of vegetarianism and "compassionate, ecologically sound living."

Otterwise, P.O. Box 1374, Portland, Maine 04104. Written for kids who are interested in protecting animals and the environment.

Vegetarian Gourmet, P.O. Box 7641, Riverton, New Jersey 08077-7641. Recipes for meatless cooking.

Vegetarian Journal, P.O. Box 1463, Baltimore, Maryland 21203. Published by the Vegetarian Resource Group.

Vegetarian Times, P.O. Box 570, Oak Park, Illinois 60303. One of the oldest, most established vegetarian magazines. Covers all aspects of vegetarianism, including lots of recipes and cooking tips.

Vegetarian Voice, P.O. Box 72, Dolgeville, New York 13329. Published by the North American Vegetarian Society.

Veggie Life, 1401 Shary Circle, Concord, California 95418. Recipes, plus tips on organic gardening.

WRITE

The Vegetarian Resource Group sponsors an annual essay contest on any vegetarian issue. To enter, send a 2–3 page essay to P.O. Box

1463, Baltimore, Maryland 21203, by May 1 for that year's contest. Winners receive a savings bond. Include your name, age, school, and name of your teacher.

Let your representatives in Washington know how you feel about grazing rights for cattle ranchers in the west. Speak out about the humane treatment of animals. Write the U.S. House of Representatives, Washington, D.C. 20515; U.S. Senate, Washington, D.C. 20510.

SHARE

Perhaps the best way to spread the word on vegetarianism is to share your good food. Don't miss a chance to bring an interesting, tasty meatless dish to a potluck or family dinner. Preaching your views usually doesn't go over, but when people are interested and ask for information, be sure to direct them to some good sources.

Source Notes

Chapter 1: Introduction

Krizmanic, Judy. "Here's Who We Are," *Vegetarian Times,* October 1992, pp. 72–90.

Chapter 2: Demystifying Vegetarianism

Were humans meant to eat meat?

McArdle, John. "Humans Are Omnivores," *Vegetarian Journal,* May/June 1991, pp. 11–12.

Bloyd-Peshkin, Sharon. "In Search of Our Basic Diet," *Vegetarian Times,* June 1991, pp. 46–55.

Protein, B_{12}, Iron:

Robertson, Laurel, Carol Flinders, and Brian Ruppenthal. *The New Laurel's Kitchen.* Berkeley, Calif.: Ten Speed Press, 1986.

Chapter 3: A History of the Vegetarian Movement

Singer, Peter. *Animal Liberation.* New York: New York Review of Books, 1990.

Spencer, Colin. *The Heretic's Feast: A History of Vegetarianism.* London: Fourth Estate, 1993.

Akers, Keith. *A Vegetarian Sourcebook.* Denver, Colo.: Vegetarian Press, 1993.

Chapter 4: Save The Environment

Durning, Alan B., and Holly B. Brough. *Taking Stock: Animal Farming and the Environment.* Worldwatch Paper 103, July 1991.

Rifkin, Jeremy. *Beyond Beef.* New York: Dutton, 1992.

Robbins, John. *Diet for a New America.* Walpole, N.H.: Stillpoint Publishing, 1987.

Wild West Welfare:

Wuerthner, George. "The Price Is Wrong," *Sierra,* September/October 1990, pp. 38–43.

Chapter 5: Save the Animals: Ethical and Religious Arguments

Singer, Peter. *Animal Liberation.* New York: New York Review of Books, 1990.

Akers, Keith. *A Vegetarian Sourcebook.* Denver, Colo.: Vegetarian Press, 1993.

Chapter 6: Stop Factory Farming

Singer, Peter, and Jim Mason. *Animal Factories.* New York: Harmony Books, 1990.

Singer, Peter. *Animal Liberation.* New York: New York Review of Books, 1990.

Robbins, John. *Diet for a New America.* Walpole, N.H.: Stillpoint Publishing, 1987.

Robbins, John. *May All Be Fed.* New York: William Morrow and Company, 1992.

Rifkin, Jeremy. *Beyond Beef.* New York: Dutton, 1992.

Spencer, Colin. *The Heretic's Feast: A History of Vegetarianism.* London: Fourth Estate, 1993.

Chapter 7: Save Your Health

The American Journal of Clinical Nutrition 59, No. 5 (S) (May 1994). Supplement: Vegetarian Nutrition.

Robbins, John. *Diet for a New America.* Walpole, N.H.: Stillpoint Publishing, 1987.

Rifkin, Jeremy. *Beyond Beef.* New York: Dutton, 1992.

Akers, Keith. *A Vegetarian Sourcebook.* Denver, Colo.: Vegetarian Press, 1993.

China Study:

Brody, Jane. "Huge Study of Diet Indicts Fat and Meat." *The New York Times,* May 8, 1990, p. C1.

Cancer:

Barnard, Neal D., M.D. "The Edge Against Cancer," *Vegetarian Times,* October 1991, pp. 18–21.

Slaughterhouse Conditions:

Robbins, John. *Diet for a New America.* Walpole, N.H.: Stillpoint Publishing, 1987.

Rifkin, Jeremy. *Beyond Beef.* New York: Dutton, 1992.

Fish:

Williams, Gurney III. "What's Wrong with Fish?" *Vegetarian Times,* August 1995, pp. 54–59.

"Is Our Fish Safe to Eat?" *Consumer Reports,* February 1992, pp. 103–112.

Chapter 8: Save the Children: Can the World Afford a Meat Habit?

Durning, Alan B., and Holly B. Brough. *Taking Stock: Animal Farming and the Environment.* Worldwatch Paper 103, July 1991.

Singer, Peter. *Animal Liberation.* New York: New York Review of Books, 1990.

Lappé, Frances Moore. *Diet for a Small Planet.* New York: Random House, 1991.

Robbins, John. *May All Be Fed.* New York: William Morrow and Company, 1992.

Chapter 9: Take Control of What You Eat

Robbins, John. *Diet for a New America.* Walpole, N.H.: Stillpoint Publishing, 1987.

Robbins, John. *May All Be Fed.* New York: William Morrow and Company, 1992.

Farm Animal Reform Movement (communication with staff members).

Dealing with Family/Social Situations:

"The Care and Feeding of Vegetarians," brochure published by the North American Vegetarian Society.

Chapter 10: A Crash Course in Nutrition

The American Journal of Clinical Nutrition 59, No. 5 (S) (May 1994). Supplement: Vegetarian Nutrition.

Johnston, Patricia K., Alla Haddad, and Dan Sabate. "The Vegetarian Adolescent." *Adolescent Medicine* 3, No. 3 (October 1992).

"Position of the American Dietetic Association: Vegetarian Diets." *Journal of the American Dietetic Association* 93, No. 11 (November 1993).

"Good Nutrition: A Look at Vegetarian Basics," brochure published by the North American Vegetarian Society.

Lappé, Frances Moore. *Diet for a Small Planet.* New York: Random House, 1991.

Robertson, Laurel, Carol Flinders, and Brian Ruppenthal. *The New Laurel's Kitchen.* Berkeley, Calif.: Ten Speed Press, 1986.

Chapter 11: Real Food for Real Vegetarians

"Heart Healthy Eating Tips." Brochure published by *Vegetarian Journal.*

"Eating Well—The Vegetarian Way." Brochure published by the American Dietetic Association.

For Further Reading

Akers, Keith. *A Vegetarian Sourcebook.* Denver, Colo.: Vegetarian Press, 1993.

A good overall introduction to vegetarianism in its many aspects. Includes a concise history of vegetarianism and a thorough discussion of the ethics of eating animals for food.

Lappé, Frances Moore. *Diet for a Small Planet.* New York: Random House, 1991.

The book that converted thousands of people (your parents, maybe?) to vegetarianism in the 1970s. Lappé, who is not a total vegetarian herself, gives a smart, level-headed perspective of meat eating and its effect on the world. Includes recipes.

Rifkin, Jeremy. *Beyond Beef.* New York: Dutton, 1992.

In this well-documented account, Rifkin details the production of beef, the cultural reasons behind beef eating, and the toll beef production takes on our environment and health.

Robbins, John. *Diet for a New America.* Walpole, N.H.: Stillpoint Publishing, 1987.

Robbins is impassioned, and some readers might not like his touchy-feely tone. Still, he's got good information about how our eating habits are shaped, an overview of the disastrous health consequences of a meat-based diet, and the straight dope on factory farming.

Sinclair, Upton. *The Jungle*. 1906; reprint, New York: Penguin Classics, 1985.
The original horror story about the meatpacking industry. As disturbing and effective today as when it was first published in 1906.

Singer, Peter. *Animal Liberation*. New York: New York Review of Books, 1990.
One of the few philosophers to consider the plight of animals and our responsibility to them, Singer gives a spirited argument against "speciesism." Also includes a brief history of vegetarianism. Not beach reading.

Singer, Peter, and Jim Mason. *Animal Factories*. New York: Harmony Books, 1990.
A thorough look at how animals are raised for food.

Spencer, Colin. *The Heretic's Feast: A History of Vegetarianism*. London: Fourth Estate, 1993.
One of the first and most comprehensive studies of the history of vegetarianism. A good read.

Index

About the Author

Jan Parr is a writer and editor living in the Chicago suburb of Oak Park. She received a B.A. in journalism from the University of Missouri and an M.A. in writing from the University of Iowa. She has worked as a writer or editor for a number of publications, including the *Kansas City Times*, *Forbes* magazine, *Chicago* magazine, and *Vegetarian Times*.